The A⌐

Kyo

methuen | drama

LONDON • NEW YORK • OXFORD • NEW DELHI • SYDNEY

METHUEN DRAMA
Bloomsbury Publishing Plc
50 Bedford Square, London, WC1B 3DP, UK
1385 Broadway, New York, NY 10018, USA
29 Earlsfort Terrace, Dublin 2, Ireland

BLOOMSBURY, METHUEN DRAMA and the Methuen
Drama logo are trademarks of Bloomsbury Publishing Plc

First published in Great Britain 2022

A catalogue record for this book is available from the British Library.

A catalog record for this book is available from the Library of Congress.

ISBN: PB: 978-1-3503-5650-4
ePDF: 978-1-3503-5651-1
eBook: 978-1-3503-5652-8

Series: Modern Plays

Typeset by Mark Heslington Ltd, Scarborough, North Yorkshire
Printed and bound in Great Britain

To find out more about our authors and books visit
www.bloomsbury.com and sign up for our newsletters.

NEW EARTH

The Apology

By Kyo Choi

First performed at the Arcola Theatre on 15 September 2022

A New Earth Theatre production in association with
Arcola Theatre and The North Wall. Developed with support
from the National Theatre

N⩵W ⩵ARTH

New Earth Theatre presents and develops work with British East and South East Asian (BESEA) artists that asks key questions of identity, of the world we live in and our place in that world.

We produce touring plays and readings across the year, nurture BESEA* talent through our Academy acting and writing courses and Professional Writers Programme, as well as bring artists to communities, museums and schools.

*We use the term British East and South East Asian to mean people of the following descent: Brunei, Burma, Cambodia, China, East Timor, Hong Kong, Indonesia, Japan, Laos, Macau, Malaysia, Mongolia, North Korea, Philippines, Singapore, South Korea, Taiwan, Thailand, Vietnam and their diasporas.

These people remain severely underrepresented in the arts in the UK.

www.newearththeatre.org.uk
@NewEarthTheatre

The Apology was created with support from Arts Council England and the British Korean Society

 Supported using public funding by **ARTS COUNCIL ENGLAND**

 British Korean Society

Cast (in order of appearance)

Kwon Bok-Hae	**Jessie Baek**
Han Min	**Kwong Loke**
Kim Sun-Hee	**Sarah Lam**
Priyanka Silva	**Sharan Phull**
Jock Taylor	**Ross Armstrong**
Han Yuna	**Minhee Yeo**

Creatives

Written by	**Kyo Choi**
Directed by	**Ria Parry**
Associate Director	**Emily Ling Williams**
Set Designer	**TK Hay**
Costume Designer	**Erin Guan**
Lighting and Video Designer	**Gillian Tan**
Composer and Sound Designer	**Jamie Lu**
Movement Director	**Jennifer Fletcher**
Dramaturg	**Caroline Jester**
Additional Dramaturgical Support	**John Hoggarth**

Production

Production Manager	**Josephine Tremelling**
Stage Manager	**Alexandra Kataigida**
Lighting Programmer	**Luca Panetta**
Video Programmer	**Benet Doeringer**
Set and Costume Work Experience	**Yijing Chen**
Community Engagement Assistant	**Madeleine Baker**
Community Engagement Assistant	**Heeyeon Park**
Production Assistant	**Jeni Seo**
Production Work Experience	**Yuino Tokumaru**
Press	**Kate Morley PR**

Special thanks to:
Christina Anderson, Tzer Han Tan, Mei Mac, John Hollingsworth, David Yip, Dinita Gohil, Liz Sutherland-Lim, Nathaniel Tan, Sadao Ueno, Leo Wan, Rachael Cowie, Jerry Cox, eStage, Suki Mok, Soho Theatre, Emily McLaughlin, Nina Steiger, Stewart Pringle and the National Theatre New Work department, Lucy Park, Derek Man, Louis Smith

Jessie Baek | Kwon Bok-Hae

Jessie Baek was born and raised in South Korea. She is of both North and South Korean heritage, and grew up near the border. She graduated from Rose Bruford College in 2017.

Theatre includes: *The Visit* (National Theatre); *Wild Goose Dreams* (Theatre Royal Bath); *One Day Maybe* (Hull City of Culture); *The Handmaiden* (Secret Cinema).

Television includes: *Bridgerton* (Netflix); *Secret Life of Boys* (CBBC).

Kwong Loke | Han Min

Kwong trained at the Guildhall School of Music and Drama. He was a founder member of New Earth Theatre and frequently runs acting workshops in East Asia.

Theatre includes: *What Remains of Us* (Bristol Old Vic); *The Great Wave* (National Theatre); *Pah-la, New and Now, You For Me For You* (Royal Court); *You Never Touched the Dirt* (Royal Court at Edinburgh); *Labour of Love* (Noël Coward, West End); *Summer Rolls* (Park Theatre, Bristol Old Vic); *Dear Elizabeth* (Gate Theatre); *The Lulu Plays* (Almeida Theatre); *Hiawatha* (Bristol Old Vic); *The Changeling* (Finborough Theatre); *Rashomon, Blue Remembered Hills* (New Earth Theatre UK tour); *The Magic Paintbrush*, *The Snow Lion* (Polka Theatre).

Television includes: *Gangs of London* (HBO-SKY); *Biff and Chip* (CBeebies); *The Feed* (ITV Amazon); *As Time Goes By (BBC One); Love Hurts (BBC One); The Knock* (Bronson/Knight Productions); *The Monkey King* (Hallmark Entertainment).

Radio includes: *At Sea on Inya Lake; Another Land; Our Father the Mountain; Joy Luck Club.*

Sarah Lam | Kim Sun-Hee

Theatre includes: *Rice* (Orange Tree Theatre/ATC); *Paradise, World of Extreme Happiness, Magic Olympical Games* and *Lost Worlds* (National Theatre); *Snow in Midsummer* and *Poppy* (RSC); *La Cage aux Folles* (Park Theatre); *Richard II* (Shakespeare's Globe); *The Country Wife* (Southwark Playhouse); *Sergeant Ola and his Followers, Cries from the Mammal House* and *Top Girls* (Royal Court); *Factors*

Unforeseen (Orange Tree Theatre); *Mail Order Bride* (Northampton Theatre Royal); *All the President's Men* (West End) and *Chimerica* (Almeida Theatre/West End).

TV includes: *Maryland*, *Back to Life*, *Casualty*, *Holby City*, *Sherlock*, *Two Thousand Acres of Sky*, *Top Girls*, *Angels* and *Howard's Way* (BBC); *Lucky Man* (Sky); *Frank Stubbs Promotes* (ITV); *No Problem!* and *Brookside* (Channel 4).

Film includes: *China Connection*.

Radio includes: *One*, *Inspector Chen*, *Higher*, *Brief Lives*, *Eye of the Day*, *World Writing*, *A Many-Splendoured Thing*, *Different Planes*, *The Joy Luck Club*, *Words on the Night Breeze*, *Beyond the Takeaway*, *Chinese Whispers*, *Devils in the Glass*, *A Sensitive Season* and *Top Girls* (BBC).

Sharan Phull | Priyanka Silva

Theatre includes: *Everybody's Talking About Jamie* (UK tour); *Bend It Like Beckham: The Musical* (Phoenix Theatre); *The Show Must Go On! Live* (Palace Theatre); *2020: Collection 1 Monologues* (Tara Theatre); *Halls The Musical* (Turbine Theatre); *Am Dram: A Musical Comedy* (Curve Theatre); *Pink Sari Revolution, Scrooge: The Musical* and *The Importance of being Earnest* (Curve Theatre); *Kings of Broadway Concert* (Palace Theatre); *Romeo and Juliet, Macbeth* (National Theatre).

Workshops include: *Run, Rebel* (Pilot Theatre); *Extraordinary Women* (Waterloo East Theatre); *Great British Bake Off: The Musical, The Boy in the Dress* (Royal Shakespeare Company); *The Visit* (Nottingham Playhouse); *Is She One of Us?* (Jermyn Street Theatre).

Television and radio includes: *Doctors* (BBC); *Middlemarch Monologues* (BBC Radio 3); *Back* (Big Talk Productions/Channel 4); *Cadbury Secret Santa* (VCCP).

Recording: *Bend It Like Beckham* (Original Cast Recording).

Ross Armstrong | Jock Taylor

Ross trained at RADA.

Theatre includes: *A Midsummer Night's Dream* (RSC/Garsington Opera); *Oppenheimer* and *The Shoemaker's Holiday* (RSC); *The Boss*

Of It All (Soho Theatre); *The Deep Blue Sea* (West Yorkshire Playhouse); *Antony and Cleopatra* (Liverpool Everyman); *Hamlet* (Donmar Warehouse/Broadway); *Cyrano de Bergerac* (Chichester Festival Theatre); *The White Devil* (Menier Chocolate Factory); *Hapgood* (Birmingham Rep); *Henry V* (Manchester Royal Exchange).

Television includes: *Pennyworth* (Warner Horizon/Epix); *The Letter for the King* (FilmWave/Netflix); *Chernobyl* (HBO/Sky); *Will* (TNT); *Ripper Street*, *Our World War* [Interactive], *WPC 56*, *Jonathan Creek* (BBC); *Love and Marriage* (Tiger Aspect); *Foyle's War* and *Mr Selfridge* (ITV); *DCI Banks* (Left Bank Pictures); *Titanic* (Deep Indigo/ITV); *Spooks* (Kudos).

Film includes: *The Critic* (Mark Gordon Pictures); *Decoy Bride* (Decoy Productions Ltd).

Minhee Yeo | Han Yuna

Theatre includes: *Dear Elizabeth* (Gate Theatre); *Deliverance* (Vanishing Point/Brite Theatre); *White Pearl* (Royal Court Theatre); *Under the Umbrella* (Belgrade Theatre/New Earth Theatre/Tamasha); *Mountains: The Dreams of Lily Kwok* (Royal Exchange Theatre/New Earth Theatre); *Hear Me Now* (Tamasha); *Just One More Time* (The Space, One Festival); *One Day, Maybe* (dreamthinkspeak/Hull UK City of Culture 2017); *Chinglish* (Park Theatre); *Replay* (C Venue, Edinburgh Festival); *Leodo: The Paradise* (Maro/Edinburgh Festival).

Television includes: *Strike Back: Legacy* (Sky1/Cinemax); *Cuffs*, *EastEnders*, *Out of Her Mind* (BBC).

Film includes: *Avengers: Age of Ultron*; *Kotchebi*; *A Perfect Turn*.

Kyo Choi | Writer

Kyo is a South Korean playwright and screenwriter based in London and Portugal. *The Apology* was developed as part of New Earth Theatre's Professional Writers Programme. She was selected as one of the writers on the programme to develop the play further at the National Theatre Studio. As a screenwriter, she has recently written a landmark Lunar New Year episode for *Hollyoaks* and is also working with Little House Productions on a biopic film about Wendi Murdoch. Last year, she was commissioned by the Royal Central School of Speech and Drama to write a play for a large cast, resulting in

Galápagos, performed at Bridewell Theatre in March 2022. She is currently under commission to write a new musical.

Ria Parry | Director

Ria Parry | Director

Ria is Co-Director of The North Wall in Oxford. She has produced four Fringe First Award winning plays by Gbolahan Obisesan, Paul Charlton, Marika Mckennell and Karim Khan.

Ria's previous directing work at Arcola Theatre includes *Jane Wenham: The Witch of Walkern* (Out of Joint) and *The Island Nation* (Ice and Fire).

Theatre credits include: *E8* (Edinburgh Fringe Festival); *Albion* (Bush Theatre); *Bike*, *On Golden Pond* (Salisbury Playhouse); *The Winter's Tale Re-imagined* (Regent's Park Open Air Theatre); *Mad About The Boy* (Edinburgh Fringe/UK tour); *Dr Korczak's Example* (Unicorn Theatre); *Tales of Winter* (Southbank Centre); *Crush* (Edinburgh Festival/UK tour); *Fen* (Finborough Theatre); *Love and Money* (RADA); *Spring Awakening* (LAMDA) and *Not I* by Touretteshero (Creative Associate/BAC/UK tour).

Ria was previously a Creative Producer at Watford Palace Theatre and is an alumna of the National Theatre's Step Change Leadership Programme. She was awarded the Leverhulme Bursary for Emerging Directors in 2010, becoming Resident Director at the National Theatre Studio.

Emily Ling Williams | Associate Director

Emily is currently a Headlong Origins Artist and was previously a Resident Director at the Almeida Theatre, Jerwood Assistant Director at the Young Vic and Trainee Director at Paines Plough.

Theatre, as director, includes: *The Full Works*: *The Key Workers Cycle* (Almeida Theatre); text me *when you're home*: *5 Plays* (Young Vic); *Swallow*, *16* (Lemon House Theatre); *Lucky Cigarette* (New Earth Theatre); *GYSB*, *Tuesday at the Library*, *A Perpetual State of Happiness*, *Good Trouble* (Moongate Productions); *Before You Go* (New Earth Theatre/National Theatre Studio – rehearsed reading); *Appropriate* (RWCMD); *Miss Julie* (LAMDA); *Preach* (Rose Bruford); *Turbines* (Paines Plough/ RWCMD/Gate Theatre).

As assistant director: *The House Of Shades* (Almeida Theatre); *Blood Wedding* (Young Vic); *The Meeting*, *The Chalk Garden* (Chichester Festival Theatre); *Black Mountain*, *Out Of Love*, *How To Be A Kid* (Paines Plough/Theatr Clwyd/Orange Tree Theatre); *The Island Nation* (Arcola Theatre).

TK Hay | Set Designer

TK's previous work for New Earth Theatre includes *Tsunagu/Connect*.

TK is a Singaporean theatre designer based in the UK. He trained at the Royal Welsh College of Music and Drama and won the Linbury Prize in 2019, working on *An Adventure* (Octagon Theatre, Bolton). His winning design on the show was subsequently nominated for best design at The Stage Debut Awards in 2022. He was a recipient of the Singapore National Arts Council Scholarship in 2016.
Website: tkhay.design

Erin Guan | Costume Designer

Erin Guan is a London-based scenographer and interactive installation artist from China. She has a strong interest in interdisciplinary theatre and performance making and she works across installations, plays, musicals, dance, digital theatre and devised theatre. Her work spans across intercultural performances and minority voices. Her digital artwork specialises in Augmented Reality and Virtual Reality experiences. Her VR installations *Chamber404* is exhibited in Ars Electronica 2020 x Interactive Architecture Lab, Camden People's Theatre, Vault Festival 2022 and VA Lab Taipei.

Theatre includes: *Unchain Me* (Dreamthinkspeak/Brighton Festival); *Symbiont* (Caged Bird Theatre/The Vaults); *Foxes* (Defibrillator Theatre/Theatre503); *Tokyo Rose* (Burnt Lemon Theatre); *Talk*, *The House Never Wins* (Kill The Cat Theatre); *Freedom Hi*, *Asian Pirate Musical* (PaperGang Theatre); *The Letters Project* (Gate Theatre).

Gillian Tan | Lighting and Video Designer

Gillian is a multi-disciplinary designer, working across lighting and video for various theatrical, immersive and interactive experiences.

Theatre includes: *South Pacific* (Chichester Festival Theatre/Sadler's Wells/UK tour); *The Body Remembers* (Fuel); *Black Love* (Paines

Plough/Belgrade Theatre Coventry/tiata fahodzi); *Really Big and Really Loud* (Paines Plough/Belgrade Theatre Coventry); *When The Long Trick's Over* (High Tide); *Cinderella, The Awesome Truth* (Polka); *Alyssa, Memoirs of A Queen* (Vaudeville Theatre); *Aisha and Abhaya* (Royal Ballet/Rambert); *Majestique* (Skråen); *The Song Project – Is In Our Blood* (Royal Court Theatre); *4.48 Psychosis* (revival Lyric Hammersmith/Royal Opera House); *La Soirée* (Aldwych Theatre/ Southbank Centre/Skråen); *Coraline* (Barbican Theatre/Royal Opera House); *Tamburlaine* (New Earth Theatre/Arcola Theatre); *Invisible Treasure* (Ovalhouse Theatre); *Who Do We Think We Are?* (Southwark Playhouse); *Crocodiles* (Royal Exchange, Manchester).

Film includes: *NYX and Gazelle Twin Present: Deep England*; a performance film by Iain Forsyth and Jane Pollard; and *Held Momentarily* (Royal Academy of Music).

She is also a member of the Somerset House Exchange and is the Head of Video at RADA and recently participated in the Unreal Engine Storytelling Fellowship.

Jamie Lu | Sound Designer and Composer

Jamie's previous work at the Arcola includes: *We Started to Sing* and *Broken Lad*.

Theatre, as sound designer, includes: *The Unicorn*, *What the Heart Wants*, *How to Build a Wax Figure* (Edinburgh Fringe); *Sorry We Didn't Die at Sea* (Seven Dials Playhouse); *The Blue House* (Blue Elephant Theatre); *Dirty Hearts* (Old Red Lion Theatre); *Burnout* (SHYBAIRN Theatre); *Tokyo Rose* (Southwark Playhouse/UK tour); *A Report to an Academy*, *Butterfly*, *The Most Beautiful Woman in the World* (Baron's Court Theatre); *Apollonia*, *Flowers for Algernon*, *Black Mary Poppins* (Focustage/Chinese tour); *Paper Crown* (Corbett Theatre/Bloomsbury Festival); *Wild Duck* (West Side Theatre, ET Space, China); *The Sound of Music* (Chinese tour); *Sink* (Courtyard Theatre/Edinburgh Fringe/ Southbank Centre China Changing Festival); *String* (Lion and Unicorn Theatre). As scenographer, *A Thousand Papercuts Skin Deep* (Baron's Court Theatre); *A Report to an Academy·Live* (online). As assistant sound designer, *Henry V* (Donmar Warehouse). As sound designer for audio play, *The Dream Machine* (Fizzy Sherbet).

Josephine Tremelling | Production Manager

Josephine is a production manager, lighting designer and theatre maker. She studied at Dartington College of Arts obtaining a BA Hons in Contemporary Theatre before working as a drama facilitator and co-founding inclusive theatre company Anyone Everyone and cabaret troupes The Thrill Billies and The Salacious Sirens.

After deciding to broaden her technical theatre knowledge, Josephine took the role of technician and later of production manager at the Pleasance Theatre and then as a freelance production manager and lighting designer.

Her current projects include national and international tours with Ephemeral Ensemble, Theatre Re, Tangled Feet and The Little Angel Theatre.

Theatre includes: *We Started to Sing* (Arcola Theatre) and *Hamlet* (with the National Theatre).

Alexandra Kataigida | Stage Manager

Alexandra's previous work for New Earth Theatre includes: *Forgotten* 遗忘 (with Moongate) and *Under the Umbrella* (with Belgrade Theatre Coventry and Tamasha). Previous work at the Arcola includes: *Liminal* and *Swipe*.

Theatre includes: *Into the Numbers* (Moongate); *Lautrec* (Hen and Chickens); *Money Heist: The Experience* (Fever); *Journey's End*, *After All These Years*, *When Love Grows Old* (Theatre Revival); *The Lion, the Witch and the Wardrobe* (CentreStage); *Exit the King* (Carisbrooke Castle); *Macbeth* and *Hamlet* (Icarus Theatre Collective); *Zero Down* (Theatre503); *Hood* (Soho); *iAm* (Bush); *Childsplay* (Riverside Studios); *Prince of Denmark* (National Theatre); in-person and online theatre for Shake-Scene Shakespeare, Some Kind of Theatre, 60 Hour Shakespeare, The Show Must Go Online.

As well as specialising in touring stage management, Early Modern drama and theatrical armoury, Alexandra is highly experienced in fight co-ordination for stage and screen, and has developed movement systems for portraying physical action in theatre in isolation.

arcola
theatre

Arcola is one of London's leading off-West End theatres.

Locally engaged and internationally minded, Arcola stages a diverse programme of plays, opera and musicals. World-class productions from major artists appear alongside cutting-edge work from the most exciting emerging companies.

Arcola delivers one of London's most extensive community engagement programmes, creating thousands of opportunities every year. By providing research and development space to diverse artists, Arcola champions theatre that's more engaging and representative. Its pioneering environmental initiatives are internationally renowned and aim to make Arcola the world's first carbon-neutral theatre.

The North Wall
Arts Centre

The award-winning North Wall Arts Centre opened in 2007 and brings together artists and audiences from Oxford and beyond to make, share and experience art of the highest quality. Comprising a theatre, gallery and studio spaces, the venue's public programme places an emphasis on contemporary work, amplifying diverse voices and providing a platform for untold stories.

Alongside its programming, The North Wall supports artists through its ArtsLab programme, which offers established and early-career artists the chance to develop and showcase new work through residencies, mentorship and training.

In addition to this, the venue runs a participation programme with children, young people and families at its heart; forging long-term partnerships with local schools and community groups to co-create projects which bring people together through creative opportunities.

The North Wall is grateful for the continued support of its principal sponsor, St Edward's School.

Co-Directors	**John Hoggarth & Ria Parry**
Programme & Marketing Manager	**Amy Walters**
Technical Manager	**Clive Stevenson**
Participation Manager	**Abigail Walton**
Gallery Manager	**Nicky Laird**
General Manager	**Wendy Weiss**
Associate Producer	**Amelia Thornber**
Front of House Manager	**Gabi Wilson**
Theatre Technician	**James Bailey**
Front of House Supervisors	**Guendalina Degl'inoccenti & Ethan Powell**

The North Wall Trust is a limited company and registered charity.

Registered company no: 07951538
Registered charity no: 1146851
The North Wall Arts Centre, South Parade, Oxford OX2 7JN
Tel: 01865 319 450

thenorthwall.com

@thenorthwall

The Apology

For my mother and father

Characters

Kwon Bok-Hae, *South Korean*
Han Min, *South Korean*
Kim Sun-Hee, *South Korean*
Priyanka Silva, *Sri Lankan*
Jock Taylor, *American*
Han Yuna, *South Korean*
Soldier, *Japanese*

In Korea, the family name precedes given names. Example: 'Han' is the family name of Min.

The play is set in Seoul. The timeframe is 1945 to 2018.

1945 – Min is 22 years old, Bok-Hae, 18
1955 – Min is 32, Bok-Hae 28
1965 – Min is 42, Yuna 19
1991 – Min is 68, Sun-Hee, 64, Yuna 45, Priyanka 33, Jock 41
1993 – Min is 70, Sun-Hee 66, Yuna 47, Priyanka 35, Jock 43
1996 – Jock is 46
2018 – Yuna is 72, Priyanka, 60

There are flashbacks when Bok-Hae is a young girl during wartime in Manchuria.

NB: Han Yuna was born in 1945 but her birth was registered in 1946. The text uses her registered birthdate.

Note on layout

A character may interrupt the previous character's speech. This is marked by /

Two characters may speak at the same time. This is marked by *

A character may be cut mid-sentence by the next character. This is marked by –

Author's Note

This is a work of fiction. However, it is inspired by certain persons, events and testimonies of the survivors of Japanese military sexual slavery during World War Two.

Prologue

1945. Final days of World War Two. Harbin, Manchuria. Night. Sporadic gunfire, shouting, impending doom. A cubicle covered by a dirty sheet. We see the action in silhouette through the sheet.

Soldier *Ianfu!* Smile! Might be my last time.

A girl – **Bok-Hae** *– is balled up. He kicks her.*

Soldier Ooooh, chubbier are we? Captain been fattening you up?

Bok-Hae Please, mercy. Have some mercy.

She cries.

Soldier I deserve mercy. (*He pulls down his trousers.*) I don't want to die!

The chaos gets louder. Gunfire, then a voice shouts:

'Burn everything! Kill the *Pii*! Kill all the women!'

The soldier jolts upright, his trousers round his ankles. Picks up a gun as **Bok-Hae** *cowers in fear.*

Soldier Mother, I'll see you in heaven!

He shoots himself in the head. **Bok-Hae** *screams. She sits up, her head turning frantically in all directions. Then, an abrupt silence. A pause before the next round of artillery. A bird sings loudly as it takes flight.* **Bok-Hae** *stands, listening to the bird.*

Act One

The Woman on the Tape

Scene One

1955, Seoul. Early morning, still dark. A tiny bedroom. **Bok-Hae**
lies on a floor mattress, covered, while **Min** *is getting dressed. Folded
clothes on the corner of the bedclothes.*

Min (*to* **Bok-Hae**)   And she picks out the weevils from her
bento box. Lines them up on the desk. Tells her friends *you*
put the weevils there for protein!

Bok-Hae *perhaps nods.*

Min   See how canny our little Yuna is. Just nine years old.

Very clever . . . for a girl. Mmm.

Keeps asking me to speak Japanese. (*Turns to look at his wife.*)

I said, you want to speak Japanese? Eat dolphin meat!
(*Huffs.*) Better she learns English or Mandarin. Anything but
Japanese, the devil's language.

Dressed, he stands upright to be admired by his wife.

How do I look? Smart for my first day? I have a head for
numbers, they said. Might pay for an accounting course if I
do well.

She nods her head.

You and I, we've endured the Japs, North Koreans. Two
wars! We're more than survivors. We're indomitable!

He takes **Bok-Hae**'s *hand.*

Min   Bok-Hae-ya, forsythia's in bloom.

Bok-Hae *mumbles something to him.*

Don't worry. There's barley rice-balls left and potato soup.

He strokes her head.

Yuna won't be home 'til late. She's fund-raising for a blackboard. In other words, she's out begging. Ha!

He leaves. **Bok-Hae** *remains in bed.*

She rises. She removes her nightclothes, puts on her day clothes. She folds the bedclothes and puts them in the corner. She looks at the room for the last time before leaving.

TRANSITION: 1965. **Yuna** *and* **Min** *stand before a prepared je-sa – ancestral memorial – table in* **Min***'s small flat. A photo of* **Bok-Hae** *stands at the table laden with food, fruit and soup in strict order. The photo is flanked by lit candles.*

Min *does two-and-a-half floor bows, followed by* **Yuna***, who does the same.*

Scene Two

1991. Seoul. Ministry of Foreign Affairs (M.O.F.A.) office.
Priyanka *is about to listen to a tape.* **Bok-Hae** *sits on a chair. She is not in the same scene.*

Priyanka *starts the tape. A woman speaks in Korean.*

'In 1943, I was sixteen years old. I was selling dried radish in the market. My mother was sick with bronchitis. I went alone. A man came up and offered to buy all the radish. He asked about my family. It was just me and mother.

Sun-Hee *takes over, talking to us.*

Sun-Hee   He told me about the Female Volunteer Corps, that I could be a nurse. It was the patriotic thing to do, he said. He persuaded me to go to the local police station. There . . . I was put in a cell with three other girls. A Japanese soldier came in . . . and . . . he . . . (*She cries.*) The next morning I was taken by truck to Manchuria with my cell mates. There, I was kept locked up in this . . . pig sty. I prayed the soldiers to not come to me . . . (*She looks at us.*) I try so hard to forget those times of horror.'

Lights fade on **Sun-Hee**. **Priyanka** *massages her temples.*

She jolts at a loud rapping on the door.

Priyanka   Come in.

Enter U.S. Deputy Chief of Mission to South Korea, **Jock Taylor**, *a spirited man, sharp and acerbic.*

Taylor (*extends his hand, gives her a glance over*)   Ms Silva? Jock. Jock Taylor –

Priyanka (*shakes his hand*)   Nice to –

Taylor (*still shaking her hand*)   Deputy Chief of Mission.

Priyanka (*pulls her hand away*)   Of what?

Taylor (*chuckles*)   U.S. Embassy. Second in chain of command.

Priyanka   Ah.

Taylor (*makes a welcome gesture with his arms*)   Welcome to the Land of the Morning Calm!

Priyanka   Thank you.

Taylor   Japan's Land of the Rising Sun. Stands to reason South Korea's, well –

Priyanka   Land of the Morning Calm. I know.

Taylor   As I was saying, both flags have a circle in the middle, similar grammar. According to the Japanese Diplomatic Blue Book, 'South Korea is Japan's most important neighbour that shares strategic interests'.

Priyanka   Makes sense in the current political climate.

Taylor   You'd think. But, if you took a poll today, most South Koreans loathe Japan. Only the Chinese hate them more!

Priyanka   Japan's brutal occupation. Forty-six years ago – not a long time.

Taylor   Every occupation is brutal. Like every divorce is bitter. / Hunh?

Priyanka (*puzzled*)   Do we have an appointment?

Taylor   Oh, just poppin' my head in.

Priyanka   Perhaps we can arrange a suitable time to –

Taylor   Heard a big-shot U.N. sheriff was in town.

Priyanka   I'm an independent counsel advising the U.N.

Taylor   Yeah, yeah. (*Points to tape recorder.*) See you got the tape.

Priyanka   Is that why you 'popped in'.

Taylor (*laughs*)   From the Korean Council for Justice and Remembrance for the Issues of Military Sexual Slavery by Japan. What a mouthful.

Priyanka   Someone's done his homework too.

Taylor   Nah, word gets around.

Priyanka (*glances at her watch*)   I have a meeting in, um, ten minutes.

Taylor   You're a busy woman. (*Gestures at tape recorder.*) She's a busy woman. Busy times for you women!

Priyanka *stares at him.*

Taylor   Agh, that came out all wrong. Just meant this is a uh, busy . . . for y'all, well, y'know what I mean.

Priyanka   Came out 'all wrong' alright –

Taylor   Could be anyone on that tape.

Priyanka   The Korean Council knows who this woman is. I want to meet her.

Taylor   Surprised the U.N. is interested in this.

Priyanka   Just preliminary fieldwork.

Taylor   Are you close to a mandate?

Priyanka   We've been tracking this for a while.

Taylor   Kinda like recon, huhn?

Priyanka   In your parlance, I suppose.

Taylor   Whoever she is, she ain't talking to the media.

Priyanka   I'm not media.

Taylor   Getting the U.N. Commission on Human Rights on board for a country like this? Circus in town, folks!

Priyanka   Calling them a bunch of clowns?

Taylor   No-ho-ho, sir. Ma'am.

Priyanka   Mr Taylor, for decades rumours have been swirling of Korean women abducted by the Japanese Imperial Army during the war. Parents terrified of their daughters being forced to work for the Female Volunteer Corps –

Taylor   And not a single woman speaks up.

Priyanka   Until now.

Taylor   If she's for real.

Priyanka   And why would –

Taylor   The U.S. Embassy be interested? (*Smiles.*) We're all humanitarians here.

Priyanka   But?

Taylor   No 'buts'. (*Checks his watch.*) Time for your meeting! (*Puts his hand out to shake hers. She obliges.*) Sure I'll be seeing you again.

Priyanka   Doubt it. I'm leaving tomorrow.

Taylor   You better get going then.

Priyanka   Good to meet you –

Taylor   Your little show here gets shut down if you don't get a name. The identity of this random woman.

Priyanka (*eyes narrow*)   That's more than word getting around.

Taylor   C'mon, it's the U.N., baby! Big, bloated and low on budget. Ah, who cares? Y'all have a big bulging heart. (*He winks.*) You take care now, Ms Silva.

He leaves.

Scene Three

1991. Seoul. **Min***'s modest flat. He reads the newspaper.*

Min   No . . . no, no!

Throws it to the floor. He paces, lost in deep thought. **Yuna** *enters with a wheelie cabin case, dressed in a flight attendant's uniform.*

Min   Mm, Yuna-ya. You look terrible.

Yuna   Worst shift ever. London, Dubai, Singapore, Sydney. (*Yawns.*) I'm going back to my flat for the longest sleep.

She notices the paper on the floor. Goes to pick it up. **Min** *rushes over.*

Min (*voice raised*)   I'm still reading that!

He tucks the paper under his arm. She flops on his armchair.

Yuna   Well, I was just –

Min   You need to rest. Don't bother tidying here.

He puts the paper away in the drawer of a console.

Yuna   Wanted to read that . . . Haven't read the news for weeks.

Min   Usual nonsense.

Yuna (*yawns*)   Someone on the plane told me we joined the U.N. with North Korea?

Min   Disgraceful to accept those terrorists.

Yuna (*sighs*)   Yes, *Appa*.

Min   Why don't you go back to your place?

Yuna   Thought we could eat together –

Min   No, no . . . I have leftovers from yesterday.

Yuna   Are you sure?

Min   Sure sure.

Yuna   Are you alright?

Min   Yes, why?

Yuna   You seem a little . . . on edge.

Min   Must be my new cholesterol tablets. Ha!

Yuna   Hope they're working.

Min   Working alright, medicating the elderly. Never-ending money spinner!

Yuna (*sighs*)   Can we turn on the T.V. ?

Min   I don't want to watch T.V.!

Yuna   'Everyone's Popular Songs' is on now.

Min   Pure sop.

Yuna   What? That's your favourite show –

Min   How long are you here for?

Yuna   Two days.

Min   Go and rest up.

Yuna (*takes out a box of Quality Street chocolates from her wheelie bag*)   Here.

Min   Still have the last box you bought me.

Yuna   This has lots of the ones with strawberry filling.

Min (*takes a chocolate*)   My favourite.

Yuna   Sure you don't want me to stay?

Min   Yeah yeah. Shut everything out and sleep. OK?

She leaves. **Min** *switches on the T.V. A news reporter speaks (V.O.):*

Reporter   'An elderly woman has come forward for the first time claiming to have been a sexual slave to the Japanese military during World War Two. Thousands of Korean women may have been involved –

Min *switches off the T.V.*

Min   No . . . NO!

Scene Four

Sun-Hee *talks to herself, pacing. Perhaps we see an imagined* **Bok-Hae** *separately, before she was taken away by her captors.*

Sun-Hee   I buried you. I did. I buried you . . .

— Wretched girl.

— You shouldn't have followed that man! You, a nurse! How could you possibly be a nurse? You were just a peasant girl who dreamed of being a dancer.

— Your decision, to follow that man. That was my life. My life!

— You. Ruined. Me.

— No! I don't want to hear it! Go away!

Scene Five

Seoul. **Priyanka** *is is at the airport. Her mobile phone rings.*

Priyanka   Priyanka Silva.

She listens.

What?

She listens.

This is incredible!

She listens.

I'll cancel my flight. Thank you. Uh, *kamsa-hamnida.*

She hangs up.

Fucking incredible !

She reaches into her handbag, takes out her wallet. Gazes at a photo – her sister – in a sleeve. She kisses the photo.

Scene Six

A small office at the Korean Council for Justice and Remembrance for the Issues of Military Sexual Slavery by Japan, west Seoul. **Priyanka** *is nervous, paces.*

A soft knock on the door. She opens the door. **Sun-Hee** *enters. She walks assisted by a cane, with a limp.*

Priyanka   Good morning.

Sun-Hee *nods.*

Priyanka   I understand you speak English. Thank you. For this meeting. Please.

Sun-Hee *sits, as does* **Priyanka***, opposite her.*

Sun-Hee   You are U.N. rep?

Priyanka   No. I'm a human rights lawyer, specifically women's rights. My name is Priyanka –

Sun-Hee   Women's rights? So, you not work for U.N.?

Priyanka   Well, I've been asked to come here by the U.N.

Sun-Hee Where you from?

Priyanka Sri Lanka . . . Were you expecting someone else?

Sun-Hee A man. American or English.

Priyanka I see.

Sun-Hee They no tell me you are Indian.

Priyanka (*eyes widen*) Sri Lankan. Sorry. I mean, not for being . . . never mind.

Sun-Hee What?

Priyanka I'm sorry if you were misled.

Sun-Hee Is you or your boss I talk to.

Priyanka Just me today. But my colleagues in the U.N. are very interested in what you have to say.

Sun-Hee So why they not here?

Priyanka It doesn't work that way. These situations require an independent envoy to investigate first.

Sun-Hee Eh?

Priyanka My interest is women impacted by armed conflicts. Sorry, I don't know your name.

Sun-Hee I no want to tell my name.

Priyanka OK . . . This is very brave what you are doing.

Sun-Hee I want to forget. But I can not. You understand?

Priyanka Yes –

Sun-Hee But Japanese say they not do this, this not happen. They are lying. This happen to me. And many many women.

Priyanka I'm sorry.

Sun-Hee You say sorry too much.

Priyanka   Um, could we start from the beginning.

Sun-Hee   OK.

Priyanka   I hope you don't mind if I record this conversation.

Sun-Hee *nods.*

Priyanka   Alright.

She presses the recorder. **Sun-Hee** *remembers the first day in Harbin.*

Lights fade on **Priyanka**. **Sun-Hee** *watches her younger self:*

1944. A spotlight shines on **Bok-Hae** *in rags, blood stains on her underwear. She lies on a filthy bed in a tiny dark room. A naked bulb hangs from the ceiling.*

Bok-Hae   Please . . . water.

A man's voice booms (V.O.).

Man   These are the rules of this comfort station in Harbin, Manchuria, state of the Emperor of Japan:

Admission allowed only for soldiers and officers.

Visitors must pay the fee at reception and a receive a ticket and a *sakku*.

A ticket-bearer must go to designated room.

Time limit is thirty minutes except for officers who are allowed up to one hour.

Do not drink alcohol on the premises.

Those who do not obey the regulations, and those who debase the morals, will be ordered out of the room.

Comfort women are allowed to stroll from 8 a.m. to 10 a.m. everyday.

Bok-Hae   Where am I? . . . I'm here to be a nurse.

Man *laughs.*

Bok-Hae   Please, help me. I need medicine.

Man   *You* are my medicine now.

Bok-Hae   I don't under –

Man   Shut up.

Bok-Hae   You see, I'm bleeding.

Man   How old are you?

Bok-Hae   Sixteen.

Man   So old? Never mind. *Arigatō-gozaimasu*, my Emperor!

She retreats in fear, falls on her back.

Bok-Hae   What are you doing? No, no, no! (*She screams.*)

Man   Open your legs.

Bok-Hae   No.

Man   You stupid *Pii*. I said, open your legs!

Bok-Hae   Don't, please . . . *Omma!* Help me!

Man   You know what happened to the last girl who said no? (*He laughs.*) That was fun. Too noisy though.

Bok-Hae   *Omma!* Help me! *Om-maaa!*

We are back with **Sun-Hee** *and* **Priyanka** *together.* **Sun-Hee** *is stoical.*

Priyanka   I'm sorry . . . Do you want to stop?

Sun-Hee *shakes her head.*

Sun-Hee   No . . .

Priyanka   OK. You know you can stop for a break whenever you –

Sun-Hee   They say Korean men are farmers, women are farm animals . . . we not allowed clothes when station open. From here. (*She points to her waist.*)

Priyanka   You were naked from waist down.

Sun-Hee *nods.* **Priyanka** *breathes out.*

Sun-Hee (*with disgust*)   It is honour to serve Japanese soldiers. The Emperor.

Priyanka   And were you paid?

Sun-Hee   No! We are in debt to station managers for room, food and medicine.

Priyanka   Indentured.

Sun-Hee   Prisoner.

Priyanka   Were you ever free to leave?

Sun-Hee   They torture us or shoot us if we try to.

Priyanka   I'm sorry to ask, how many soldiers were there in a day?

Sun-Hee   Twenty, thirty. Sometimes more.

Priyanka   You were expected to have sex with so many, every day?

Sun-Hee   The line outside building like at train station.

Priyanka   Were they all Japanese soldiers?

Sun-Hee   Soldiers in day, officers and captains at night.

Priyanka   Did you receive medical treatment?

Sun-Hee   Once a month. Doctor force a duck-mouth-shape metal thing inside me . . .

Priyanka   For venereal disease.

Sun-Hee   We have '606', injection. Everything is swelling and bleeding (*She wrings her hands.*) in that part . . . Hard to put injection there.

Priyanka   '606'? That's arsenic-based.

Sun-Hee   They tell us '606' we not get pregnant, also kill baby inside.

Priyanka   Did many women get pregnant?

Sun-Hee   The soldiers, some refuse to wear 'sakku' –

Priyanka   Condoms.

Sun-Hee   They beat us if we ask them to.

Priyanka   How many women were in this station?

Sun-Hee   I don't know. One hundred, maybe more.

Priyanka   Did they all join the Female Volunteer Corps?

Sun-Hee   Many. Not all.

Priyanka   The Korean Council has traced the volunteer corps to Taiwan, Thailand, Philippines, not just Korea and Japan.

Sun-Hee *shrugs.*

Priyanka   But no one has come forward.

Sun-Hee (*cries out*)   You think I am lying?

Priyanka   I believe you. (*She stands up.*) When I was little, I loved to catch frogs with my friends. With nets. We'd let them go after. One older boy, he'd catch many frogs, disembowel them alive. After, a dog or cat would go missing, they were all gutted the same way. With their hearts, lungs, kidneys, organs carefully laid out. We all knew who it was. A few years later, a girl went missing. She was found, disemboweled the same way. The boy, he ran away from the village. He would have been jailed had one of us said something.

Sun-Hee   What you talk about frogs?

Priyanka   It takes courage to speak out.

Sun-Hee   No one make this tape. Only me!

Priyanka   History is full of lone voices. It's a sacrifice, for sure . . . until one voice becomes two, a shout, a siren call.

Sun-Hee (*stands up to leave*)   I make sacrifice enough!

Priyanka   Yes . . . you have.

Sun-Hee   You want me to tell my name. Show my face.

Priyanka   On tape, you could be anyone.

Sun-Hee   If I do this, what will you do? I come here to you. But you are just one woman.

Scene Seven

Sun-Hee *wringing her hands. She remembers.*

1944. **Bok-Hae** *is dressed in a dirty nurse's uniform, her face powdered patchily in ghostly white. She sings and sways nervously to a Korean folksong, 'Doraji' (Bellflower). She is not in the same scene.*

Bok-Hae
 Do-Ra-Ji, Do-Ra-Ji, Baek-Do-Ra-Ji
 (Bellflower, bellflower, White bellflower)
 Shim-Shim-San-Chon-Eh Baek-Do-Ra-Ji
 (Deep in the mountains, White bellflower)
 Han-du Buri-Man Ke-Uh-Do
 (Lift one or two roots) . . .

As **Bok-Hae** *falters,* **Sun-Hee** *takes over. She sings louder and louder, clenching her fists. Tears flow down her cheeks.*

Sun-Hee
 Dae-Ba-Ku-Ni Chul-Chul-Chul Da-Num-Neun-Da
 (Overflowing in a large bamboo basket)

Eh-He-Yo Eh-He-Yo Eh-He-Yo
Eh-Ya-Ra Nan-Da Ji-Hwa-Ja Jo-Da
(Everything is good)
Ul-Shi-Goo Cho-Ku-Na Ne Sa-Rang-Ah
(Wonderfully good for you, My love)
Do-Ra-Ji, Do-Ra-Ji, Baek-Do-Ra-Ji
(Bellflower, bellflower, White bellflower –)

Bok-Hae *Omma*'s favourite song . . . they made me sing it in Japanese.

Sun-Hee It made no sense in Japanese . . . I haven't sung that song for years.

Bok-Hae So sing it again like you just did, old woman.

Sun-Hee For whom?

Bok-Hae Just sing.

Sun-Hee Will you dance if I do? You loved that more than anything.

Bok-Hae No. I can't anymore.

TRANSITION: 14 August, 1991. A press conference in Seoul.
Sun-Hee *faces a barrage of noisy journalists, their cameras clicking and flashing. She speaks with an unleashed fury as she tells her story in Korean.*

Sun-Hee When I was young, I couldn't come out in public like this because I was so ashamed. Now that I'm old, I don't care about the shame. I'm not afraid anymore to tell you all that I was taken by the Japanese army as a sex slave, denied a normal life . . . Is this within the realm of possibility? To be raped repeatedly from when I was sixteen years old? And just as despicable is that the Japanese government knew about it. Our own government knew about it. Do you know this? You'd expect them to stand up for us. But instead, they didn't want to hear anything from us. So we hid ourselves and cried day and night. All we could do was shed tears silently. We had no one to talk to. I'm talking today. Because I'm afraid that no one will do it after I die.

I exist now. Don't tell me that I didn't exist before.

We see photos of women survivors who have come forth since 1991, from China, South Korea, Taiwan, Philippines, Thailand, Papua New Guinea.

1992. The Wednesday Demonstration. Chanting. A protest in front of the Japanese Embassy in Seoul. Hundreds of women – survivors of World War Two, students – join the 'halmonis', the grandmothers known as 'comfort women'.

TRANSITION: 1993. A broadcast: 'Japan's Chief Cabinet Secretary, Yohei Kono, has made a landmark statement regarding the so-called "comfort women" during World War Two. He states, "The Government of Japan has conducted a study that indicates comfort stations were operated in extensive areas for long periods . . . it is apparent there existed a great number of comfort women . . . in many cases, they were recruited against their will through coaxing, coercion. Undeniably, this was an act with the involvement of the military authorities of the day . . . The Government of Japan would like to extend its sincere apologies . . ."'

Act Two

Never Rest in Peace
(All of this Act is set in 1993)

Scene One

Seoul. **Sun-Hee** *walks with a limp on stage. A large box sits on the floor. Her head is shaven. She is dressed in Buddhist grey robes. She opens the box to reveal a lump of clay. She looks around. Sees a chair on the side. Drags the chair over. She looks for something, leaves offstage. When she returns with a sculpting knife, she finds* **Bok-Hae** *sitting on the chair.* **Sun-Hee** *gasps.*

They look at each other. Lights fade.

TRANSITION: Late morning. **Min**'s *small apartment. He's dozing in an armchair. Enter* **Yuna**, *in a flight attendant's uniform with a cabin wheelie bag. She surveys the room, frowns. She removes her shoes and approaches* **Min**. *She arches forward and looks at him, with sorrow.*

Yuna   *Appa. (She waits for him to wake, without touching him.) Appa?*

Min *(his eyes open and shut slowly, he is somewhat disoriented)* Oh . . . hmm.

Yuna   Wake up.

Min *(he sleep-talks)   Yuh-bo*, where have you been?

Yuna   It's me . . . Yuna.

Min   Sun is setting . . . Mountain will fill with shadows. You don't like shadows.

Yuna   *Appa*, please.

Min   Were you collecting autumn leaves?

She holds back emotion.

Min (*his eyes come into focus*)   Yuna?

You look just like your mother!

He breathes deeply, still in the grip of his slumber.

Yuna   You were dreaming.

Min   Was I? I don't remember.

Yuna   Something about leaves changing colour . . . You were happy.

Min   I don't have happy dreams.

Yuna   You're awake now.

Min   But I want to return to my dream!

A drawn-out silence.

What are you doing here anyway?

Yuna   Told you I was coming back for *Omma*'s *je-sa* ceremony.

Min   It's been almost forty years since your mother left . . .

Yuna *looks at the je-sa table by the wall, set with fruit and rice cakes.*

Yuna   You've started preparing for tonight.

Min   Mmmm.

Yuna (*beat*)   Shall I make some tea?

Min   She was getting cold . . . / If I could only remember –

Yuna   It's hot in here. I'll make ginseng tea.

Min (*cries out*)   Why does everyone want to feed me ginseng? Disgusting.

Yuna (*smiles; he is back to form*)   I'll mix in honey and pine nuts.

Min   So you can disguise the taste?

Yuna   You still have that honey I got from the Pyrenees?
The *organic* one.

Yuna *walks to the kitchenette, downstage left.*

Min   Organic honey? As opposed to what? I read about
seedless grapes. How can fruit be a fruit without seeds?
What next – peaches without kernels?

Yuna *returns empty-handed.* **Min** *reads his book.*

Yuna   The teapot –

Min *continues to read.*

Yuna   Can't find it.

Min   Mm?

Yuna (*she sits on the floor*)   What have you been doing, *Appa*?

Min *continues reading.*

Yuna   I haven't seen you for a few weeks.

Min   Are you worried I might be going senile too?

Min *puts down his book.*

I was at the doctor's for some stupid routine check-up –

Yuna   For what?

Min   She said, 'Grandfather Han, do you know who
Reagan is?'

Yuna   Ronald Reagan?

Min   Looked at me like I was crazy. You know Reagan is
losing his marbles.

Yuna   Why would she ask you that?

Min   Said to that quack, Reagan? Of course I do. Star Wars.

Yuna (*slightly worried*)   *Well, he was an actor before.

Min   *That upstart, started scribbling furiously in her notepad.

Yuna   Mostly in cowboy Westerns –

Min   His Strategic Defence Initiative was called Star Wars. Ha!

Yuna (*laughs*)   Guess that shut the doctor up.

Beat. **Yuna** *looks round the room.*

What have you done with the dining table and chairs?

Min   Don't need it. See? I've got more room to exercise.

He gets off his chair and does a vigorous circuit round the room, thrusting his shoulder blades up, then out and down. Flops back on his chair.

Yuna   This place . . . looks so unwelcoming.

Min   You don't live here anymore.

Yuna   I'm nearly fifty, *Appa.*

Min   Still flying round the world serving wine and cheese to foreign businessmen.

Yuna   I told you, I'm chief purser now. I manage the crew. More than just catering.

They sit in silence. **Yuna** *is afraid to ask any more questions. She gets up and brings her wheelie bag. She unzips it and takes out a photo album.*

Min   You remembered!

He carefully inspects the photos from the first page.

Your mother was from the famed North Hamgyong-do in North Korea – *Where the most beautiful women are from.

Yuna (*rolls her eyes*)   *Where the most beautiful women are from.

He continues to scan the photos. He points at one.

Min   This photo, I like this photo of me.

Yuna   With the hydrangeas behind you –

Min   My dream! She was collecting leaves. (*Excitedly.*) Blow up this photo.

He takes the photo out of the album sleeve and gives it to her.

Yuna   Brighten up this room.

Min   It's not for the apartment.

Yuna   Where is it for then?

Min   You'll need it one day.

Scene Two

Seoul. An interview room in M.O.F.A. **Sun-Hee** *is in Buddhist robes.*

Priyanka   Sun-Hee. My, how you've changed.

Sun-Hee   You have good eyes.

Priyanka   How is this life? Quiet and calm?

Sun-Hee   Eh? I am very noisy nun!

Priyanka   Ahh. A campaigner now.

Sun-Hee   I just fly back from Tokyo.

Priyanka   Tokyo?

Sun-Hee   Many right wing fans there. They come to airport to spit at us, call us whores. I shout back: 'Show respect to Zen Buddhist nun!'

Priyanka   Was this for your lawsuit?

Sun-Hee (*nods*)   We are three women who go.

Priyanka   I read about it. It's amazing.

Sun-Hee   We will not win. It's OK. People must know what they did to us.

Priyanka   Kono's statement has caused quite a storm.

Sun-Hee   Not enough! His apology is not endorsed by the Diet.

Priyanka   You mean it's not an official apology that their parliament has approved.

Sun-Hee *nods.*

Sun-Hee   And what you are doing here?

Priyanka   To lay the groundwork for a full U.N. investigation.

Sun-Hee   What means 'lay the groundwork'?

Priyanka   To prepare.

Sun-Hee   Prepare for what?

Priyanka   A full investigation.

Sun-Hee   You do this for two years already!

Priyanka   We don't have a full mandate yet: Violence Against Women. I'm hoping this report will convince them.

Sun-Hee   I made the decision to go public.

Priyanka   And now, hundreds of women all over Asia have come out.

Sun-Hee   Now you keep promise! You promised justice! Or this all for nothing!

Priyanka *is at a loss for words. She knows this will be a lengthy drawn-out process.*

TRANSITION: **Sun-Hee** *starts sculpturing the clay. She is angry.*

Scene Three

Same day. Late afternoon. M.O.F.A. interview room. A loud rap on the door.

Priyanka   Come in.

Enter **Jock Taylor**.

Priyanka   You! Still here?

Taylor   What can I say? They don't call it a hardship posting for nothing.

Priyanka   I like Seoul. Makes a nice change for me.

Taylor   So you're back for more.

Priyanka   Just arrived last night.

Taylor   Suits here are all whispering 'bout it over their bento boxes.

Priyanka   Only a follow-up trip.

Taylor   Wanna health tip? – Avoid the canteen here.

Priyanka   Beats my usual lentil soup.

Taylor   Man, s'all chilli and garlic, then more garlic and chilli. Er, perhaps you're used to that . . . You from India, Pakistan?

Priyanka   Sri Lanka. We can handle our chilli and garlic.

Taylor   Sounds like you went to Oxford though.

Priyanka   Bristol, actually.

Taylor   Huh.

Priyanka   Amazing people still think there're only two universities in England.

Taylor   Where is, uh, Bristol?

Priyanka   Southwest, river Avon?

Taylor (*amazed*)   It exists? Where King Arthur died?

Priyanka   That's Avalon. And he doesn't die –

Taylor   I'm a Dartmouth man myself. (*Beat.*) Didn't make the cut for Harvard.

Priyanka (*beat*)   Thank you . . . for coming by –

Taylor (*his demeanour shifts from the jovial*)   Ms Silva, what you're doing here . . .

Priyanka   Yes?

Taylor   I, er, commend you.

Priyanka   Haven't started yet.

Taylor   Can't be easy for a woman tackling this issue.

Priyanka *looks at him with mild incredulity.*

Taylor   Comfort women . . . and all that.

Priyanka   'Comfort women' . . . You and I both know that's a misnomer. Military sexual slavery is a much more accurate and appropriate terminology. And it's been under our radar far too long.

Taylor (*claps his hands*)   Bravo! First female Armstrong.

Priyanka   Don't exaggerate –

Taylor (*mutters*)   Boy, does it feel like the moon here.

Priyanka   I've been chasing this for a while.

Taylor   Say, what were you doing before?

Priyanka   Amnesty International. Beijing.

Taylor   Beijing?

Priyanka   Observing the One-Child Policy –

Taylor   And before?

Priyanka   Is this a job interview?

Taylor   Looking for one?

Priyanka   No!

Taylor   Relax . . . just getting to know you.

Priyanka   Perhaps you want to see my C.V.

Taylor   Before Beijing, Director of the International Centre for Ethnic Studies, as you still are. Ethnicity, women and human rights, with special interest in female fighters of the Tamil Tigers.

Priyanka   Hunh. Do you work for the CIA too?

Taylor (*laughs*)   Nah, they mostly recruit from state colleges.

Priyanka   What else do you know about me. Am I . . . a cat or dog lover?

Taylor   Wasn't in the file. If I had to guess, neither.

Priyanka   Go on.

Taylor   People like you hate being tied down, even to a chihuahua.

Priyanka   People like me?

Taylor   Justice warriors.

Priyanka   That's one way to describe it.

Taylor   Look, Priyanka – can I call you that? A beautiful name. (*She ignores the compliment, simply nods.*) – This is an emotive issue in South Korea.

Priyanka   Potentially two hundred thousand women forced into Japanese military rape centres? I'd say so.

Taylor   A hypothetical number.

Priyanka   Hard to prove when most of them were killed at the end of the war.

Taylor   Objection, your honour! Again, conjectural.

Priyanka   Just a number. A number that everyone wants to forget, right?

Taylor   'Til recently. You know about the Wednesday Demonstration?

Priyanka   The protest outside the Japanese Embassy here. Yes, I do.

Taylor   Every Wednesday since 1992! Not saying a bunch of old ladies and their school-girl fan base are gonna storm the U.S. Embassy any day soon . . .

Priyanka   A bunch of old ladies.

Taylor   You know what I mean.

Priyanka (*shakes her head*)   Sorry, your politics are not within my purview.

Taylor (*snaps back*)   Should be within your *pur-view*.

Priyanka   This is a human rights issue, Mr Taylor. Not a political issue.

Taylor   To quote that feminist – whatever her name was – 'everything is political'.

Priyanka   You're mixing quotes. 'That feminist' wrote 'The personal is political'. And her name *is* Carol Hanisch.

Taylor   No flies on you. (*Smiles patronisingly.*) How long you here for?

Priyanka   Surely you know already.

Taylor   Three days.

Priyanka *looks at him wryly.*

Taylor   Habit. Pretending not to know what I know.

Priyanka   Must be tedious.

Taylor (*shrugs*)   Good lie detector if anything.

Priyanka   I bet.

Taylor   There's a restaurant outside, specialising in tofu stew, loaded with garlic, chilli, some chopped octopus tentacles, a raw egg. Clear out your sinuses.

Priyanka   Sounds amazing.

Taylor   Tomorrow lunch?

Priyanka   I'll try.

Taylor   Look forward to it.

He opens the door to leave.

Priyanka   Mr Taylor?

Taylor   Hm?

Priyanka   Why?

Taylor   Told you – canteen here is abominable.

Priyanka   Not that why.

Taylor   Don't follow.

Priyanka   The background search. On me?

Taylor   You're on my turf, Armstrong. (*Smiles.*) I got on this moon first.

Taylor *leaves.* **Priyanka** *sits down.*

Priyanka   Armstrong. My arse.

Scene Four

Min's *apartment. Early evening. A small portable radio is on. A lacquered low-table with a black-framed photo of* **Bok-Hae** *placed on the edge, unlit candles on each side.* **Yuna** *prepares the ritual table to commemorate her mother's death at midnight. She comes and goes as she brings the food. She pauses to listen to the radio, turning up the volume.*

Radio: A panelist speaks. 'This Kono apology is significant but it's not an official apology and no mention of war crimes. This is unacceptable. Women from all over Asia and Europe but predominantly from Korea were kidnapped or lured from their villages and sent to Japanese outposts in Manchuria, Taiwan and their Southeast Asian colonies . . .'

Min *enters. He watches his daughter somewhat entranced by what she's listening to. He switches off the radio.*

Min   Where did this come from?

Yuna   I was listening to that. It's my portable radio.

Min   What for?

Yuna   What *for*? No T.V., no radio, you don't even read the papers anymore.

Min (*looks at table*)   Why are you setting this so early?

Yuna   What do you mean? The memorial for *Omma* is tonight.

Min (*checks his watch*)   Eh? . . . Look at the time.

Yuna *goes to switch the radio back on.*

Min   No! Leave it off.

Yuna   It's interesting.

She goes to turn the radio back on.

Min   I said leave it off!

(*Regarding the table.*) No *gulbi*?

Yuna   They're talking about the women, *our* women . . . during the war.

Min *huffs dismissively.*

Yuna   *Appa* –

Min   Garbage.

Min *picks up the framed photo from the table.* **Yuna** *thinks. Something has lodged in her mind.*

Min   This was taken just after you were born.

Yuna   Strange . . .

Min   Hm?

Min *still holds the photo.*

Yuna Did you hear what she said . . . Those places . . .

Min Admittedly, a son would've been good.

Yuna (*she is distracted*)   . . . What?

Min I was happy regardless but, a son is a son.

Yuna (*half-listening to* **Min**) They don't accept Kono's apology.

Min Never trust a politician when he's handing out free rice cakes.

Yuna It's a huge story –

Min There's no story to follow!

Yuna They're talking about the Japanese military sending our women to something like 400 stations all over China, Southeast Asia. And New Guinea. Do you know how far away that is, *Appa*? By ship in those days?

Min *remains silent.*

Yuna And . . . and there is a written record . . . it said, in one station there was 'one woman for every 100 soldiers'. I just can't . . .

Min It's war, Yuna.

Yuna To be raped even once in a lifetime, but this . . . all day . . . for years. How can you *live* after that?

She is entranced by a thought that is still knotted in her head.

Min (*he takes photo in one hand and brandishes his free arm*) When we were colonised, you think those dolphin-eaters viewed us as human?

Yuna I don't care about all of that . . . (*She is still in the grips of a thought.*)

Min   What's wrong with you? (*Shakes his head.*) And they think I'm senile.

Yuna   *Appa* . . .

Min   We all suffered, men and women alike –

Yuna   Actually, they said one of the largest outposts was in –

Min   It's a deliberate ploy. Reminder of our subjugation –

Yuna   *Manchuria.*

Min   Your head is still in Greenwich Mean Time or wherever you flew in from.

Yuna (*snaps back*)   My head is just fine, *Appa*.

Min   Why don't you rest more?

Yuna *stares at her father, opens her mouth to speak but she is afraid.*

Yuna (*fear in her eyes*)   *Omma* . . . *She* worked there . . .

Min (*a shift in tone*)   So?

Yuna   She worked in Manchuria.

Min   Don't be ridiculous.

Yuna   She did though.

Min   That was a long time ago.

Yuna   During the war.

Min   This is *some* jet-lag . . . Really, I think *you* need some ginseng tea.

Yuna   Didn't she?

Min (*holds the photo in both hands and looks at it as he speaks*) War is a knife in your gut.

Yuna   *I know it was a hard time –

Min   *Either you pull it out or push it in deeper.

Yuna   What was *Omma* doing in Manchuria?

Min   Stop this nonsense. Show some respect!

Yuna *stares at her father.*

Min   On this of all days.

Yuna *is surprised by* **Min**'s *anger. He puts the photo back on the table, strides to the door, puts his shoes on.*

Yuna   Where are you going?

Min   To get the dried fish. Can you prepare the rice please? Or maybe you should go back to your own apartment and sleep off this fog in your mind.

He leaves. **Yuna** *sits, lost in thought. Then she lights the candles on the table and stares at the photo of her mother. She slams the photo down.*

Scene Five

Seoul. M.O.F.A. interview room.

Priyanka   When the Japanese surrendered and you were liberated –

Sun-Hee   Why you not read my testimony! Soldiers go crazy. Go into every room with rifles and swords. Shoot and kill many girls. I pretend I am dead.

Priyanka   Sun-Hee, I have to verify certain things.

Sun-Hee   People only want bad stories.

Priyanka   I'm sorry?

Sun-Hee   How many times Japanese rape you? Is true they boil sick girls and you eat? Can you have children? Reporter in Tokyo ask me this. Can you have babies? Why you not kill yourself if it so bad?

Priyanka *is at a loss for words.*

Sun-Hee   Are you speaking truth or are you after money because you are poor low class whore? You will ask me that too?

Priyanka   No. I'm here to listen.

Sun-Hee   When the war ended, this man . . . A good man. I am very sick. He take me to hospital, come every weekend to see me and bring Asian pear . . .

She holds back tears.

I never even hold hands with a boy before. You understand?

TRANSITION: Spotlight on **Sun-Hee** *sculpting. She suddenly sees* **Bok-Hae**.

Spotlight on **Bok-Hae**. *She is utterly worn down, dirty and broken.*

Bok-Hae   *Omma* . . . I'm sorry I couldn't contact you . . . You must have worried but I'm . . . alive.

Sun-Hee   *Omma* . . . I'm sorry I couldn't contact you . . . You must have worried but I'm . . . back.

They drop their heads.

Bok-Hae   There was no money to spare, the hospital paid so little. I'm so sorry . . .

Sun-Hee   There was no money. They locked me up in a tiny room. The drunken soldiers were the worst.

They crumple to their knees.

Bok-Hae   I'm fine . . . Just so exhausted . . .

Sun-Hee   I wanted to kill myself . . . but you would have suffered more, not knowing what happened to me.

They break down in tears.

Bok-Hae   *I missed you so much. I wish I hadn't gone.

Sun-Hee   *You don't know how much I missed you, *Omma*.

Scene Six

Evening. **Min** *sits on his chair, puts his chopsticks down on a tray on the floor, a half-eaten kim-bap on the tray.* **Yuna** *sits on the floor. The conversation is strained, in light of previous scene.*

Yuna   You know, in London, any where in Europe really, they only sell long-grain rice. Uncle Ben's rice –

Min   Un-cle Ben . . . Does he own many rice fields in Europe?

Yuna *(laughs)*   No, it's a brand.

They scratch their heads when you ask for short-grain rice.

Min   Unbelievable.

Yuna *(checks her watch, sighs)*   Four more hours to go.

Min   A proper *je-sa* should be around midnight, not this modern nonsense of doing it at dinner because it suits lazy people.

Yuna *(looks at the half-eaten roll)*   Didn't you like my kim-bap?

Min   It's . . . edible. Not quite like the rolls that the *ajumma* in the market makes.

Yuna *(tries not to take offence)*   True, her acorn jelly tastes authentic.

Min   I'm trying to persuade her to make kimchi stew. / Can't be that difficult.

Yuna   Even I can make that!

Min   You have many talents, Yuna, but cooking isn't one of them.

They laugh.

Yuna   *Appa,* shall I cut your hair?

Min   Has it been three months already?

Yuna   Think so.

Min *looks pleased, the meal has gone well.*

Min   I'll get the sheet and scissors.

They shift the je-sa table to make space. **Min** *goes to his bedroom and comes out with a folded sheet and scissors, a comb, a mirror. A semblance of normalcy. He places the chair in the middle of the room and sits.* **Yuna** *places the sheet with a hole in the middle over his head. She combs his hair down, starts to snip around his ears.*

He closes his eyes and starts humming, then singing, in poor but comical mimicry, 'That's All Right', by Elvis Presley. **Yuna** *smiles.*

Min   Oh, she loved Elvis.

Yuna   Yes.

Min   She'd clap her hands when he finished singing that on the radio.

Yuna (*she pauses the cutting*)   You know, that was the only time she'd laugh, was actually happy. Listening to the radio.

Yuna *resumes cutting.*

Min   Be careful behind my ear.

Yuna   Stop moving then.

Min (*picks up the mirror*)   Mmm.

Yuna (*stops cutting. She talks almost to herself, not facing* **Min**) She was . . . sad. All the time. I'd come home from school and see her in bed.

Min   She took good care of us. / It's all she wanted.

Yuna   I used to wonder how the food got there –

Min   She had a frozen shoulder for a long time –

Yuna   You and I went to the market on the weekends . . .

Min   Are you cutting my hair or not?

She faces her father.

Yuna   Who sits on the sofa knitting when the sun is out?

Min   Not this again, Yuna!

Yuna   The cushion was so worn where she sat in the same place . . .

Min   It's your idea to cut my hair!

He removes the sheet in anger. He remains seated whilst **Yuna** *stands.*

Min   Are you having boyfriend problems again?

Yuna   No!

Min   Sounds like it.

Yuna   Is it . . . are you getting rid of things that remind you of *Omma*?

Min   Why would I do that?

Yuna   So why does this room look like a monk cave?

Min *sighs.*

Yuna   Or is it something else . . .

Min   I won't live forever, you know.

Yuna (*fear in her voice*)   Did that doctor tell you something?

Min   That child-quack? I can run rings around her any day.

Yuna   So, everything is fine with you.

Min   Everything is fine.

Yuna   You're not going to die any day soon. (*Smiles.*) / Unless my cooking kills you.

Min   I didn't say that.

Yuna (*beat*)   What did you just say?

Min *is silent.*

Yuna (*shakes her head*)   Not funny, really isn't.

Min   I'm not joking.

Yuna   You shouldn't say things like that . . . it's cruel.

Min   To continue living, how cruel is that for an old man?

Yuna   Are you in some kind of trouble? In debt?

Min (*laughs*)   If I were, I'd jump off a building. Isn't that what all these corporate leaders do these days?

Yuna *massages her temples, shakes her head.*

Yuna   It's not funny! You know what, I'll quit my job, stay here with you.

Min   That's not healthy. For either of us. You would drive me crazy.

Yuna   Why don't we freshen up here with new wallpaper? / Look, it's peeling off –

Min   New wallpaper won't give me a new outlook on life.

Yuna   How about a cruise to Hokkaido? It's beautiful with volcanoes, hot springs.

Min   I'd rather be shot in the trenches than go sightseeing in Japan!

Yuna   I don't understand . . .

She's about to cry.

It's because of *Omma*, isn't it?

Min   She's been gone for so long.

Yuna   Can I tell you something, *Appa*?

Beat.

Yuna   I'm . . . glad.

Min   What?

Yuna   That she's gone.

He slaps her. **Yuna** *is stunned. Nurses her cheek.*

Min   Don't talk about your mother like this.

Yuna   You know what I used to think? That she was my step-mother.

Min *remains silent.*

Yuna   All those excuses: 'Your mother can't come to the school play but she's proud you're doing the lead role of *Shimcheong*.' Or 'Your mother isn't well, so let's go on that trip another time . . .' I can go on and on.

Min   Don't be insolent, not tonight. Not when we're about to do the ceremony.

Yuna   Her eyes . . . so cold . . .

Min   War . . . it's like a knife thrust in your gut . . .

Yuna   She never loved me, Appa! / Admit it –

Min   No! She did. She did.

Yuna (*she starts to cry*)   You're still protecting her.

Min   I'm not! I . . .

Yuna   From what?

Min (*shouts*)   I couldn't protect her!

Yuna (*seizes on a thought, whispers*)   Does this have something to do with Manchuria?

Min   Don't you dare. Dishonouring her –

Yuna   You know what I learnt from all those foreign businessmen I serve wine and cheese to? They talk. They don't hide. They don't give a dried fish about honour. So, let's talk, *Appa*.

Min   Some things are better left unsaid.

Yuna   She's dead! I don't even know how she died. And now this nonsense with you making some crazed plans.

What about me? You've made some pact with her, haven't you? Tell me! You know what, I won't let you. I really don't care about her. She never loved me, you know that and I know that.

She gets up and rushes to the je-sa ceremonial table.

Min   What are you doing?

Yuna *sweeps her arm across the je-sa table, all the food crashes to the floor. The photo of* **Bok-Hae,** *too, comes crashing down, breaking.*

Min   *Yuna! Have you gone crazy?

Yuna   *I'm not doing this *je-sa*! You hear me? I'm not doing it! Because I hate her! I hate her! I'm glad she's dead!

Min *closes his eyes, his head hung in defeat. A long beat. He takes out an envelope from his shirt pocket.*

Yuna   What . . . What's that?

Min   You want to know what she was doing in Manchuria?

Yuna *reaches out for the envelope but* **Min** *clutches it firmly in his hand.*

Min   So does the U.N. (*Beat.*) She can never rest in peace!

Act Three

The Bigger Issue

Scene One

Spotlight on **Sun-Hee**. *She is humming, sculpting using wire and metal-tip tools. The clay is taking on a crude form of a small girl sitting on a chair.*

Lights fade. 1945 (post-war). A spotlight on **Bok-Hae**, *heavily pregnant.*

She is cleaning the floor of a small room with a rag. Suddenly, she is seized with pain. She is going into labour.

Bok-Hae   No . . . no . . .

She gasps with pain. Collapses to the floor.

She punches her stomach over and over again.

Dokkaebi . . . dokkaebi . . . goblin child . . . hateful goblin child.

She stops. She gets up and glares at **Sun-Hee**.

Bok-Hae (*to* **Sun-Hee**)   Give me that.

She grabs the metal-tip tool from **Sun-Hee**'s *hand. She stabs the face of the sculpture repeatedly.*

Bok-Hae   You stupid girl! You stupid stupid girl! I don't want your goblin child!

Sun-Hee *screams in anguish. A baby's cry is heard.*

Scene Two

1993. *M.O.F.A. office. Noon.* **Priyanka** *sits at her desk. A knock on the door.* **Taylor** *enters with two plastic bags of takeaway food.*

Taylor   Beautiful day, Armstrong!

Priyanka   This is . . . un-statesmanly.

Taylor   Mama said never skip the most important meal of the day.

Priyanka   Might've meant breakfast?

Taylor   S'all the same thing. Rice for breakfast and hey, more rice for lunch!

Priyanka   And to think you're a diplomat.

Taylor   You always take things so literally?

Priyanka   Thought the plan was to eat out?

Taylor   Place is crawling with college kids on dates.

Taylor *unpacks the food and lays it out on the table.*

Taylor   Couldn't bring the tofu octopus stew, too messy.

Priyanka   Looks delicious.

He splits his disposable wooden chopsticks and carves them against each other to remove the splinters. She observes him.

Priyanka   What's in this?

Taylor   A whole universe of nutrients you won't find in a KFC family bucket.

Priyanka   Hunh.

They eat for a while.

Priyanka   (*a little unnerved that* **Taylor** *isn't talking, eating with gusto*)   Do you like working in Seoul, Mr Taylor?

Taylor   Jock.

Priyanka   Jock.

Taylor   Mmm.

He continues eating.

Priyanka   So . . . what do you do for fun?

Taylor (*whilst eating*)   Ka-ra-O-kay.

Priyanka   A man of many talents.

Taylor *continues enjoying his meal.*

Priyanka (*tries another tack*)   You know they don't even acknowledge that word.

Taylor   Hunh?

Priyanka   Slavery.

Taylor   C'mon! We're having such a pleasant meal.

Priyanka   Just checking I hadn't lost you in all the chilli and garlic.

Taylor   Mama also said don't talk unpleasantries at the table.

Priyanka   Ohhhh.

Taylor   Enjoying your meal?

Priyanka   So enjoyable.

Taylor (*wipes his mouth with a paper napkin, he's finished his meal,* **Priyanka** *hasn't*)   Say, you always deal in weighty words: humanitarian, injustice, slavery –

Priyanka   Oh, are we allowed to talk now?

He gestures with his arms: 'of course'.

Priyanka   Kono's statement. Never refers to it.

Taylor   Dear Lord!

Priyanka (*finishes her meal*)   Delicious. Thank you.

Taylor   He apologised. In a public statement.

Priyanka   You and I both know that's not enough.

Taylor   In diplomacy, you never get what you want. In fact, you don't even aim for it. You aim for an . . . approximation.

Priyanka   How do you aim for an approximation of reparation?

Taylor (*laughs softly*)   There you go again, Armstrong, with those big words.

Priyanka   Do you think this is droll?

Taylor   Humour is often an expression of grim optimism.

Priyanka   I prefer hope. Simple optimism.

Taylor   Look, this wasn't flagged as a crime during the Tokyo War Crimes Tribunal.

Priyanka   Thanks to your General MacArthur.

Taylor   Ah . . . the great General MacArthur. Such a sad demise –

Priyanka   Wrapped up the Tokyo Trial with minimum sentencing. Left off the Emperor for starters. No wonder they continue to defy –

Taylor   You're conflating this with a whole other thing –

Priyanka   No, I'm not. That's the legacy: evading state responsibility.

Taylor   Alright, alright, let's back up a little here.

Taylor *piles up the plastic bowls and cutlery and puts them back in the plastic bags. He speaks as he's doing this.*

Your apology comes with a lotta strings attached.

Priyanka   In your warped diplomacy world.

Taylor   There are bigger issues at stake here.

Priyanka   Like what?

Taylor   Think about it. These victims are mainly from South and North Korea, China.

Priyanka   Other countries too –

Taylor (*waves a hand dismissively*)   Let's focus on China for a moment.

Priyanka   Ah. The 'China threat'.

Taylor   And North Korea? Can't even talk in your sleep there. There won't be any humans left if they develop their ballistic missiles.

Priyanka   You sound anxious. In my experience, an anxious nation is often a dangerous nation.

Taylor   We're in the midst of a significant shift in the geopolitical paradigm.

Priyanka   The what? Who's talking big words now.

Taylor   We're building an alliance here, a powerhouse of Asian-Pacific economies that can rival China, Russia –

Priyanka   Ohhhh . . . these women are in your way.

Taylor   Look, I get it. Your time has finally come. (*Throws his arms in the air.*) Human rights just got a whole lot sexier! You're a god-damned inspiration to my daughters. If I had any.

Priyanka *huffs.*

Taylor   Here's the thing: Countries don't apologies for war. We don't apologise for Hiroshima and Vietnam, just like no Serb is ever going to apologise for ethnic cleansing. Germany, even Japan are exceptional exceptions.

Priyanka   'Wartime exigency' over-rules human rights, right?

Taylor   Impressed you know that term.

Priyanka   And who writes that rule book?

Taylor   Yeah, yeah, a bunch of old Ivy League men . . .

Priyanka   These women are mostly in their sixties now. And probably hundreds all over the region who still won't talk about it.

Taylor *sighs.*

Priyanka   You want another fifty years of silence.

Taylor   In fifty years, they'll all be dead!

Priyanka (*shocked*)   What?

Taylor   What – isn't that the truth?

Priyanka   Thank you for lunch, Mr Taylor.

Taylor   Guess that's my cue to leave.

Taylor *gets up to leave, he takes the plastic bags. He turns to* **Priyanka** *before opening the door.*

Taylor   All I'm asking you is to look at this big thriving region, the *Tiger* economies. The future belongs here. Let bygones be bygones.

Taylor *leaves.*

Scene Three

Min*'s apartment. Early afternoon.* **Yuna** *comes out of her bedroom. She looks around for her father. The apartment is empty. She is alarmed.*

Yuna *Appa!*

Silence. She hurries to his bedroom. She returns to the sitting room. She rushes to the front door when **Min** *walks in.*

Yuna   Where've you been?

Min   Exercising. Isn't that what you've been badgering me to do?

Yuna   Oh . . . good.

Min   Worried I ended up like a mackerel on ice in the market?

Yuna   Please . . . don't talk like that.

An awkwardness between them.

I slept in . . . Past noon already.

Min   It's fine.

Yuna   Appa, when are you going to meet with the U.N. investigator –

Min   I'm supposed to be there tomorrow morning.

Yuna   So soon? (*Beat.*) Were you even going to tell me?

Min   I did, didn't I?

Yuna   I read in the paper about her. She's a human rights lawyer from Sri Lanka. Big deal she's here . . .

Yuna *holds back tears.*

(*Almost whispers.*) She'll ask you about *Omma*?

Min   I suppose.

Yuna   How long . . .

Min   What?

Yuna   Was she in Manchuria?

Min   Nearly two years.

Yuna *does an intake of breath.*

Min   Your mother was a strong woman.

Yuna   No one can be that strong . . . no one.

Min *sits, his head bowed. A prolonged moment.*

Yuna   Why didn't you tell me?

Min   I promised her I wouldn't.

Yuna's *expression hardens.*

Yuna   Why would she leave her mother behind? Did she go alone, were there other women who went with her? Did they ever reach this hospital . . . or were they sent straight to, to work in those camps?

Min   I don't know . . .

Yuna   She was just a child . . . unless . . . she was abducted.

Min   No! She wasn't! She told me.

Yuna   I'm coming with you. To meet this U.N. woman.

Min   No, you're not.

Yuna   I'm her daughter.

Min   You're not coming.

Yuna   Show me the letter.

He goes to his bedroom, offstage. Returns with the letter.

Min   Here!

Yuna (*reads it*)   This is just a summons.

Min   Exactly.

Yuna   It doesn't even mention her name.

Min   I . . . didn't notice.

Yuna   Maybe, one of the women knew *Omma*, because you're her husband . . . I can help you. She'll probably be speaking in English –

Min   I'm not going.

Yuna   What?

Min   I'm not going.

Yuna   Yes, you are.

Min   No, I'm not.

Yuna   *Appa*, you are going.

Min   This is my business, mine alone.

Yuna   Your business . . . All that time . . .

Min   What?

Yuna   You let her suffer.

Min   Are you blaming me now?

Yuna   There were doctors who could've helped her.

Min (*mutters*)   Like she was some crazed woman.

Yuna   You weren't physically violated day in and day out!

Min   Don't!

Yuna   Don't speak of what she went through?

Min   Oh, I should have stuck to my plan.

Yuna   No – you don't get pity now.

Min   You want your old father to die a self-inflicted death.

Yuna   So you won't have to talk about the great shame of our family!

Min   How could she have even walked on the street if everyone in the whole neighbourhood knew? Tell me! You're so smart and Westernised, tell me!

Yuna   She didn't though . . . she was mostly at home.

Min   Humans are so quick to judge inhumanity. Let them live through it first!

Yuna *doesn't respond.*

Yuna-ya?

Yuna   She killed herself, didn't she? Is that a source of shame too?

Min *stays silent.*

Yuna   You'd rather take this secret to the grave.

Min   The dead don't speak.

Yuna   Is that what the Japanese taught you?

Min *is shocked.*

Yuna   Don't you see? *You* have to speak for her now.

Min   No!

Yuna   If you don't . . .

Min   If I don't, are you threatening me now?

Yuna   You're a coward. I'm ashamed to be your daughter.

Beat.

Min   I'm sorry, Yuna-ya.

Yuna (*looks away*)   It's too late. For that.

Min   You are my precious daughter.

Yuna   Stop with the sentimentalities.

Min   Can you forgive your old father?

Yuna   I don't know . . .

Min   I'm willing to pay the price.

A moment of silence.

Yuna   That doesn't pay the price, does it?

Min   What?

Yuna   Your one life. It doesn't pay the price.

Min *remains silent.*

Yuna   *Omma* wasn't the only one.

Scene Four

M.O.F.A. interview room. **Min** *speaks English with a stilted American accent.*

Priyanka   Good morning, Mr Han. Thank you for coming in.

Min *looks at her impassively. He speaks contemptuously.*

Min   When the Ministry asks you, you don't say no.

Priyanka   I see you haven't asked for a translator.

Min   My English is good. My Japanese is perfect.

Priyanka   Where did you learn English?

Min   Self-taught. You never know who will win war.

Priyanka   Impressive you've maintained it.

Min   I speak English to old fools at my local club. Easy pocket money.

Priyanka   You're a resourceful man.

Min *shrugs.*

Priyanka   Do you mind if I record this conversation?

Min   What you will do with recording?

Priyanka   I'm not here to be a whistle-blower.

Min   Eh?

Priyanka   To expose you.

Min   So . . . you no mention my name?

Priyanka   Not if you wish.

Min   Mmm . . .

Priyanka   This is not a criminal investigation.

Min   So . . . everything I say . . . is confidential?

Priyanka   Yes.

Min   Like Catholic confession. Good.

Priyanka   Can I start the recorder?

Min   No.

Priyanka   Alright. Han Min, what was your job during the war?

Min   I worked in shoe factory in Busan –

Priyanka   Forgive me, I said during the war. You weren't drafted. That's unusual.

Min *doesn't respond.*

Priyanka   Did you work *for* the Japanese military?

Min   No!

Priyanka   For whom then.

Min   The police.

Priyanka   The Korean police.

Min   Of course.

Priyanka   Who presumably were collaborating with the Japanese during the occupation.

Min   I don't know.

Priyanka   You've been named by some women who've come forward as former military sexual slaves. They identified you as a recruiter who promised them jobs.

Min *doesn't respond.*

Priyanka   Were you aware of what happened to these young women?

Min   I heard.

Priyanka   You heard. From whom?

Min   The soldiers, those *jjokpari!*

Priyanka   What does that word mean? I've heard it used before.

Min   It means people with split feet.

Priyanka   Sorry?

Min   Like sheep or goat.

Priyanka   Oh . . . cloven hooves. Uh-huh.

Min   That's how the Japanese walk, eh?

Priyanka   So you understood what was happening.

Min   Not in the beginning.

Priyanka   At some point, you did.

Min   My job is just to find them.

Priyanka   When did you start?

Min   Emm . . . 1942.

Priyanka   How many have you recruited?

Min   I don't know . . . Don't remember.

Priyanka   Five? Fifty? Five hundred?

Min   Maybe.

Priyanka   Could you be more precise?

Min   I don't know!

Priyanka (*sighs*)   Mr Han. I know this is uncomfortable but if you're going to talk like a schoolboy, I might as well send you home.

A long pause.

Min   I am happy to go home.

Priyanka   I'm sure that's not what the Ministry want to hear.

Min (*beat*)   I can tell you what I did not do.

Priyanka   OK.

Min   I did not drive in countryside looking for girls in the fields, OK? I did not go on village raids. I did not kidnap any girl. I did not hurt any family members who tried to stop it. I did not kill anyone!

Priyanka   These were well-known orchestrated –

Min   I know what you are trying to do.

Priyanka   And what is that?

Min   Try to make me confess that I am a mercenary. A traitor!

Priyanka (*sighs*)   We have photos, documents. But very little on the actual recruitment process. All we have is testimonies of the survivors.

Min   I can not help you.

Priyanka   I think you can. (*Beat.*) When Korea was under Japanese occupation and especially during the war, it must have been extremely hard to make a living. Was it the money, were you blackmailed into sourcing the women –

Min (*beat*)   They take my sisters if I don't do it.

Priyanka   I see.

Beat.

Who else was involved in the trafficking?

Min   You are the investigator! Why don't you investigate instead of asking me to give you names?

He stands up to leave.

Enough! I go home.

Priyanka   Mr Han! (*Beat.*) I've read your file.

Min *turns around.*

Min My file?

Priyanka Yes. Please, sit down.

Min *stands in his place.*

Priyanka Your wife. Her name was on the register of women at the time of liberation from a garrison in Harbin, Manchuria. It operated one of the largest Japanese slavery camps in China.

Min My wife is no longer with us.

Priyanka I know and I'm sorry. (*Beat.*) You have a daughter. Yuna.

Min She has nothing to do with this investigation. Nothing!

Priyanka Your wife was pregnant at the time. You married her despite her condition, raised a daughter who bears your name. I wanted to speak with you. You, in particular. What you did . . . is incredible.

Min *is shaken. He breaks down.*

Min I am not a good man . . .

Priyanka *waits for him to regain composure.*

Priyanka Please, help me understand for the sake of all the other women.

Min (*he breathes in deeply*) The Imperial Army, they don't want to recruit. No good for Army to be looking for girls. You understand?

Priyanka *nods.*

Min Same as the comfort stations. Run by private operators, pay license and tax.

Priyanka Koreans?

Min Sometimes. Sometimes, Japanese.

Priyanka   And how were you involved?

Min   They tell the village leaders, police and schools, we protect your family if you find girls.

Priyanka (*gasps in disbelief*)   The schools?

Min   They are the worse, indoctrinate girls to join the Volunteer Corps, to help in factories, hospitals. Not even voluntary, you have to join under National Labour Service. But many girls end up . . .

Priyanka   Is this the labour law that empowered the Japanese to draft civilian workers?

Min   Maybe . . . I don't know.

Priyanka   And the raids? What were you doing if you weren't part of it?

Min (*whispers*)   I help organise them.

He lowers his head in shame.

You said everything is confidential.

Priyanka   Yes.

Min (*beat*)   The Japanese issue travel permit to mobilise women. They control the military. Our government know everything. But the big problem now is noisy Korean women's groups. Before women nice and quiet. Our government very happy to leave this alone. Same for Japanese. Big shame culture. They are silent and venomous race. Why you think they apologise like a snake?

Germans say sorry because they feel guilt for doing something very bad. Not the Japanese. Only shame for being caught doing something very bad.

Priyanka (*ponders this*)   And what about the Americans?

Min   Eh! They don't care. As long as they are lion of the jungle.

Priyanka Are you not angry? How your wife, your country's women suffered?

Min Do you know how many Korean men were forced to fight for the Japanese during the war? You ever hear about how they suffer? No! They erased our language, our culture, the whole history of these events.

Priyanka I do know. My family name is Silva, a Portuguese name. Sri Lanka was colonised too. First Portugal, then by the Dutch, then the English.

Min I take them all instead of Japanese!

Priyanka Maybe it's your turn to talk. About the suffering.

Min You don't understand. Park Chung-Hee? We lived sixteen years under this military dictator. From 1963 to 1979.

Priyanka He has quite a record.

Min He tortured and killed many people in opposition. But I vote for him again and again because he was great leader. From ashes of war, Korea is now eleventh largest economy in world. Because of Park!

Priyanka Your point is . . .

Min Human rights – means nothing when you're starving. Crazy western idea!

Priyanka I see.

Min Feed stomach first, then spirit can dance.

Priyanka Is that a Korean saying?

Min No. My saying. If not Japanese, it is Chinese or Russians! Or North Korea! We are surrounded by vampires! Violence . . . what it means to be Korean. What makes us strong!

Priyanka So . . . you forgive the Japanese?

Min   Eh? I hate those dolphin-eaters more than anyone!

A long pause.

He takes out his wallet and shows her a black and white photo of a row of 'comfort women', one heavily pregnant. Besides them sits a grinning soldier.

Priyanka (*gasps*)   Is this your wife? The pregnant one?

Min *doesn't speak.*

Priyanka   This is . . . horrific.

Min   Look at back of photo.

Priyanka (*turns it around*)   'Korean comfort women.' It's written in English.

Min   By American military photographer.

Priyanka (*beat*)   They all knew.

She hands back the photo. He puts it away.

Min   Why don't you ask Yanks about comfort station near Tokyo that closed a year after war ended? For G.I.'s! Cost half a packet of cigarettes to get a ticket.

Priyanka   What? In Tokyo?

Min   Not just Japanese raping our women. Americans raping their women.

Priyanka   Why didn't you say, do something?

Min   I don't want revenge. I don't want justice. I want to live and die in peace.

Priyanka (*beat*)   Doesn't your daughter deserve the truth?

Min *thinks for while. Doesn't respond.*

Min   Can I go now?

Priyanka   Mr Han, would I be able to hold on to that photo? You'll get it back.

He shakes his head, bows curtly to **Priyanka***, leaves.* **Yuna** *is waiting outside the interview room.*

Yuna   *Appa*, are you alright?

Min   Mmm. Yuna-ya. I'm hungry.

Yuna   How did it go? Did you have a translator?

Min   Useless translator.

Yuna (*smiles*)   What did she ask you?

Min   Not about Reagan.

Yuna   Seriously, are you OK?

Min (*looks at her*)   Yuna-ya . . . I . . .

He thinks hard.

I told her everything. I told her that . . . that . . .

Yuna   What, *Appa*? What?

A charged moment. Will **Min** *tell her that* **Sun-Hee** *is her mother? Before he can answer though,* **Yuna** *hugs* **Min** *who stands limply.*

Yuna   It's OK. You can tell me later. We have plenty of time.

Min *wraps his arms around her. Lights fade. When they go up again,* **Min** *is hugging* **Bok-Hae**. *She is half-naked, bloodied, bruised as she was in the final days of the war. When they disembrace, he is shocked. He jolts back.*

Bok-Hae   I love this time of year when the leaves change colour.

Min   No . . .

Bok-Hae   *Yuh-bo*, have you forgotten me already?

Min   What . . . who –

Bok-Hae   Wake up from your dream, old man.

TRANSITION: As **Min** *and* **Yuna** *leave M.O.F.A. building,* **Sun-Hee** *walks toward them.* **Min** *and* **Sun-Hee**'s *eyes lock. Both are stunned.* **Sun-Hee** *sees* **Yuna**. *Her gaze drops. They pass each other.*

Scene Five

M.O.F.A. interview room. **Sun-Hee** *is in a state of shock.*

Priyanka   Sun-Hee, I wanted to see you before I leave, to thank you . . . What's wrong?

Sun-Hee   Oh. I . . . have to tell you . . .

Priyanka   What is it? Are you alright?

Sun-Hee   My real name . . . is not Kim Sun-Hee.

Priyanka   It's fine. So many other women –

Sun-Hee   The man with daughter.

Priyanka   Han Min? You know him?

Sun-Hee   Yes . . . I do.

Priyanka   Did he recruit you? Is that the man?

Sun-Hee   No . . .

Priyanka   How do you know him?

Sun-Hee   He save me.

Priyanka (*stunned*)   Were . . . you pregnant at liberation?

Sun-Hee   How you know?

Priyanka   I saw a photo, probably a coincidence. That man. He's your . . .

Sun-Hee   Husband . . . yes.

Priyanka *breathes out deeply.*

Sun-Hee   Every time I see my daughter's face, I see those soldiers . . .

Sun-Hee *weeps.*

Priyanka   Sun-Hee, listen to me. It's not your fault.

Sun-Hee   When I become nun, it is to clean. Their sins. My sins.

Priyanka   You are happy in your shelter.

Sun-Hee   Yes.

Priyanka   That's what matters, OK?

A long silence.

You have the supporters you need.

Sun-Hee   They are my family. The House of Sharing.

Priyanka   The shelter the monks offered to the survivors.

Sun-Hee   Yes. I like the monks . . . No dangerous men.

Priyanka   They're amazing to do this.

Sun-Hee   The monks are very good. They teach me art.

Priyanka   Art?

Sun-Hee   Monks in Korea are all artists. (*Leans in.*)
Unsuccessful artists. They write, paint, make pottery and
sculpture.

Priyanka (*smiles*)   Really?

Sun-Hee   I do sculpturing now.

Priyanka   I hope to see your work one day.

Sun-Hee   Lady, I hope your report will change Japanese
government.

Priyanka (*beat*)   I'm not sure it will, to be honest.

Sun-Hee   But you are here on important U.N. mission!

Priyanka   It's only a report. A start though, recognition of
how much you have suffered.

Sun-Hee   No! We want action. Full apology, children in
Japan to know what happen in the war, their government
are bad people, liars, treat women like slaves.

Priyanka   I know –

Sun-Hee   What you are here for if no action?

Priyanka It's the beginning. One day, it'll come –

Sun-Hee This is waste of time! (*Shouts suddenly.*) The *FUCKING BASTARDS!*

Priyanka *puffs air in surprise*

After war, I hear G.I.s speak many bad words: jackass, shit-heads, son of a bitch . . . *MOTHER-FUCKERS!*

Priyanka Sun-Hee, I promise you, it's not a waste of time.

Sun-Hee You tell your U.N. boss this: Every time I see the Japanese flag, I don't see a sun. I see blood.

TRANSITION: **Sun-Hee** *walks to the unfinished sculpture on a chair. A nineties pop song blasts. Young* **Bok-Hae** *appears on stage in a bling outfit. She does a dance break joyfully and with oblivion to the music. She smiles at* **Sun-Hee** *and gestures for her to join.* **Sun-Hee** *looks bewildered but then catches* **Bok-Hae**'s *rhythm of freedom and ease. She dances too, very awkwardly but with a loose abandonment. Their arms interlock until* **Bok-Hae** *releases the lock and shimmies off stage.*

Sun-Hee Come back! Please, come back.

Sun-Hee *stares. She places her hands on her face, then her arms, breasts, thighs, she examines her hands as though she sees how aged she is.*

Oh . . . If only . . .

She gazes at the sculpture. Shapes it. She starts singing Do-Ra-Ji loudly, defiantly, as she recreates the young girl she once was.

Scene Six

M.O.F.A. interview room. **Priyanka** *sits listening to an archive tape (V.O.).*

Interviewer Please state your name and situation during the war.

Angus   Er, yeah. My name is Angus McVeigh. I joined the Australian army in 1942. Six months later, I was captured by the Japs and sent to Changi POW camp. To work on the Thai-Burma Railway, y'know, the Death Railway.

A knock on the door. **Taylor** *pops his head around the door.*
Priyanka *stops the tape. Beckons him in with her hand. She places a finger on her lip to silence him. They both listen to the tape.*

Interviewer   You said there were women on that train to Banpong.

Angus   That's right. We were packed about thirty in a rail truck. The heat. Stench. Pure hell. The comfort girls, they were in the next carriage.

Interviewer   How did you know they were comfort women?

Angus   The guards called them, agh, can't remember the Jap word . . . meant horse food . . .

Interviewer   Do you know what they were doing there?

Angus   'Hospital staff.' (*Huffs.*) And they weren't women. These were kids in Red Cross uniforms, like my daughter when she goes to dress-up parties.

Interviewer   Who interviewed you?

Angus   Some Yank.

Interviewer   Do you remember what you said about the women?

Angus   Yeah. I said, 'You don't want to know about the girls in the truck?'

Interviewer   What did he say?

Angus   'Girls in the truck?' That's all.

Interviewer   He didn't have any follow-up questions?

Angus   Nah. Wasn't interested in the girls. Just wanted to hear about what the Japs did to us. How many died, starved or were beaten to death.

Interviewer   What happened to the women?

Angus   Dropped off in the jungle . . . (*Beat.*) little girls crying in the middle of nowhere.

Priyanka *stops the tape. Looks up at* **Taylor**.

Taylor   Breaks my heart.

Priyanka   You know what surprises me? So little about this in any Allied archives.

Taylor   5,424,000.

Priyanka   Sorry?

Taylor   Estimated number of civilians alone killed by the Japanese.

Priyanka   A numbers game now is it?

Taylor   I'm just putting things in perspective.

Priyanka   I'm starting to think you're spying on me.

Taylor   Nah, too old for those kinda games.

He slumps on a chair.

There were Korean collaborators you know . . .

Priyanka   I know. Just interviewed one.

Taylor   Good to explore all the angles.

Priyanka   Like buried war archives? Lots of angles there.

Taylor   There were political complications –

Priyanka   Nothing complicated about good ol' fashioned sexism and racism.

Taylor (*sarcastically*)   Only minor things like the Cold War –

Priyanka   Always about the Fear Agenda, isn't it?

Taylor   Hell yeah. S'what drives humanity. Moment a baby is born, raised on fear. Fear it might be hungry or can't sleep.

Fear it's not smart enough or won't get a job, a house, a family. Most of all, fear it won't be safe. But that don't make for great tunes hunh? (*He sings 'Love Me Do' by The Beatles, with lyrics changed.*) 'Fear fear me do. You know that I fear you. So plea-ea-ea-ea-ea-se, Fear me do. Oh-yeah, fear me do.'

Don't you just love kara-okay?

Priyanka *rolls her eyes.*

Taylor   Seriously, there's talk about a fund to compensate the victims. What more do you want?

Priyanka   Legal responsibility.

Taylor   You crazy?

Priyanka   Am I?

Taylor   We dropped two atomic bombs on them!

Priyanka   Americans always have the final say, right?

Taylor   Look, what I said about fear. The other end of that spectrum is conciliation. (*Beat.*) Way beyond that is . . . Jesus-diplomacy: to be pacific and to forgive. Isn't that what human decency is about?

Priyanka   I'm not religious, Mr Taylor. You, of all people, should know that.

Taylor   Yeah well, I was speaking figuratively.

Priyanka   Know what I fear?

Taylor   You're gonna tell me anyway.

Priyanka   This will be relegated to historical amnesia. Isn't it bad enough that their lives are on hold, at the mercy of their former captors to validate their narrative. It's like . . . they're still *enslaved* by the past.

Taylor   You got every right to be angry. Damn it – so don't buy a Toyota!

Priyanka   If these were white American teenage girls shipped to have forced sex with Japanese soldiers, would you still be here?

Taylor *is at a loss for words.*

Priyanka   I saw a photo.

Taylor (*on alert*)   A photo?

Priyanka   Girls lined up like dirty street urchins. One heavily pregnant. A soldier grinning beside them.

Taylor   Hunh.

Priyanka   On the back was written, 'Korean comfort women'. In English. You knew then, didn't you?

Taylor   From the South Koreans? Word of caution, they like to play weak and vulnerable when it suits them. All victims do.

(*Piercing glance.*) Where's this photo?

Priyanka   Not on my person.

Taylor   Ah well . . . Without proof –

Priyanka   I'm sure you've heard about this comfort station near Tokyo? To service the G.I.s who poured into Japan when the war ended.

Taylor (*tries to conceal his surprise*)   Wha – t?

Priyanka   Shut down in 1946. Must've been? . . . round the time of your guy – MacArthur?

Taylor   Show me the file! 'Stead of shootin' the breeze.

Priyanka   I'll hand-deliver it to you one day.

Taylor (*incensed*)   Who do you think you are? The Security Council? (*Blows out air.*) Least it's got some fire power. But the U.N. Human Rights Commission that's pulling your strings. (*Laughs.*) Nothin' but a goodwill gesture. So we can all feel real good about ourselves.

Priyanka   Did I hit a nerve?

Taylor   Publish this crap, you'll never get funding for your prize mandate.

Priyanka   Sorry?

Taylor   The U.S. provides one-fifth of the entire U.N. budget.

Priyanka   All this diplomatic bluster when it just boils down to money.

Taylor (*smiles*)   Armstrong, 'there's no security in this world, only opportunity'.

Priyanka   Do you quote MacArthur in your sleep?

Taylor   Yep.

Beat.

Priyanka   So . . . was it MacArthur who struck the deal?

Taylor   What deal.

Priyanka   You protect their Emperor, mask their war crimes in return for Japan down-playing *your* crime against humanity of dropping the bombs.

Taylor (*laughs forcibly*)   You crack me up, Priyanka, you really do with your conspiracy theories.

Priyanka   Just joining the dots. Your dots. Sure explains Japan's inability to accept wartime responsibility. Because they view themselves as victims too.

He glares at her as though to strike back . . . but backs off.

Taylor   S'what happens in war. Girls get raped, babies bayonetted, mothers mourn their sons – and – daughters. (*Beat.*) Your sister, I know . . .

Priyanka   Do you now.

Taylor   Quite the activist. Runs in the family / huh?

Priyanka   'What happens in war?' You're wrong. Tigers of Tamil didn't rape as a rule. It's a calculated choice, a weapon of war.

Taylor   'A weapon of war!' That tops it all. (*He laughs.*)

Priyanka   Good to talk, Mr Taylor.

Taylor   Show's over huh? (*As he leaves.*) Listen, I'm sorry . . . Sorry to hurt your feelings.

Priyanka *strides over to* **Taylor**.

Priyanka   My feelings? They're not hurt. My feelings are incensed for women who are violated in the family, the community, for women whose bodies are usurped and controlled by mechanisms perpetrated or condoned by the State. And I sure as hell am going to keep reports coming out hard and fast until one day, a young woman trafficked, dehumanised as a sex slave in some senseless war is going to win the Nobel fucking Peace Prize.

Taylor *is touched . . .*

Taylor (*wags his finger*)   You'd be a terrible diplomat . . . y'aim too high. But you might just make a terrific astronaut. (*Nods.*) So long, Armstrong.

Scene Seven

1994. The House of Sharing. Kangwon province. A small sparse room. **Sun-Hee** *holds prayer beads. Atmosphere is charged.*

Min   How are you?

Sun-Hee   I keep myself busy.

Min   Your hair . . .

Sun-Hee   Bald is liberating.

Min   I stopped watching or reading the news since –

Sun-Hee   The day I spoke out?

Min Yes.

Sun-Hee You wanted to forget those days.

Min Yes . . . You know, I looked for you. For years . . . You just vanished.

Sun-Hee Easy to do when you're invisible.

Min Then I realised that you didn't want to be found. And with Yuna, for her sake, I said . . . I said . . .

Sun-Hee Yuna . . .

Min She's nearly fifty years old. Can you believe it?

Sun-Hee I wouldn't have recognised her.

Min Oh, she fusses over me so. Very annoying at times.

Sun-Hee I'm happy you have her. How it should be.

Min Bok-Hae-ya . . .

Sun-Hee Don't call me that. That's not who I am.

Min Whatever happened, Yuna is still your daughter.

Sun-Hee No! I stopped being a victim. I invoke and I pray and I chant. For emptiness.

Min *might cry.* **Sun-Hee** *remains silent.*

Sun-Hee For peace. For purity.

Min Bok-Hae-ya . . . please. Yuna is pure. She is the purest.

Sun-Hee Please leave.

Min *stands up to go.*

Sun-Hee And thank you for your generous donation.

Min (*turns to her, tears in his eyes*)   Peace . . . How it should be.

He leaves. **Sun-Hee** *closes her eyes. She chants the 'Om mani padme hum' ('The jewel is in the lotus') Buddhist mantra.*

TRANSITION: As she chants, a spotlight shines on a life-size clay statue. A young girl in simple Korean traditional attire, sitting on a chair gazing at us.

Then . . .

Sun-Hee *opens her eyes. She looks over; it's* **Yuna** *sitting on the chair, an imagining.*

Sun-Hee   How did you . . .

Yuna   *Annyong ha-se-yo.* How are you?

Sun-Hee   It can't be.

Yuna   You see . . . I thought you were dead.

Sun-Hee   You're not really here.

Yuna   I thought you were dead.

Sun-Hee   That woman is dead.

Yuna   I might be a bastard child, poisoned with Japanese blood, a stain on your memory . . . but you live through me, *Omma.*

Sun-Hee   Don't call me that.

Yuna   I'm sorry . . .

Sun-Hee   What do you want?

Yuna   What do I want?

Sun-Hee   Go back to your father.

Yuna   To have known you. Your favourite colour or song or what you dreamt last night. Anything. Is that too much to ask? To just talk. Talk like any two women would.

Sun-Hee   It's a luxury this, to talk. Those who can don't realise how lucky they are.

Yuna   Funny, I don't consider myself lucky.

Sun-Hee   Anyway, I've said everything I needed to say.

Yuna Not to me, you haven't.

Sun-Hee Oh, I tried. But I just couldn't, you understand? I physically couldn't open my eyes, open my mouth, open my arms to you.

Yuna Please, can you not find it in your heart to accept me?

Sun-Hee Like I said, I tried.

Yuna (*snaps*) Then you should try harder. If not then, after all these years, now. Do you want me to beg you? Like you must have done?

Sun-Hee What?

Yuna You were so cold to me. I'd say now that you were cruel. Like I meant nothing to you, like you'd wished I wasn't born. Isn't that so? You won't deny it, will you?

Sun-Hee I – I'm sorry.

Yuna I don't want your apology.

Sun-Hee You're right. It's too late for that.

Yuna So tell me one thing. How did you end up any different from . . . from them?

Scene Eight

1996. **Taylor** *stands with a thick report. He has reading glasses on.*

Taylor Special Rapporteur now? Fancy title. 'Report of the U.N. Special Rapporteur on the mission to the Democratic People's Republic of Korea, the Republic of Korea and Japan on the issue of military sexual slavery in wartime.' Finally got her fucking mandate.

For a few minutes, he skims, flicks through the pages, muttering.

'. . . Mission in 1995 on the fiftieth anniversary of the Second World War would take on particular significance . . .' blah blah blah.

Reads on. We hear **Priyanka**'s *voice:*

'. . . physically and psychologically weak state these women have been in for most of their lives as a result of enduring multiple rapes on a daily basis for many years under appalling conditions . . .'

He pauses, removes his glasses and massages his brows. Sighs. Reads on.

'. . . recruitment methods . . . private operators . . . the Japanese Imperial Army resorted to violence, undisguised force and raids . . .'

Reads on.

'. . .Wholly implausible that so many women could have created such similar stories for their own purposes.' Hmmm.

Reads on. Stops abruptly.

Holy shit! (**Priyanka**'s *voice.*) 'Government of Japan remains legally responsible for the consequent violations of international humanitarian law . . . Recognise that the systemic recruitment of women for purposes of sexual slavery should be considered –'

What? 'Should be considered a crime against humanity.' The hell?

He breathes. Shuts the report. Paces. He returns to his seat. Goes to the end of the report.

Alright. Let's get to the meat of this.

'Recommendations. The government of Japan should:

A spotlight on **Sun-Hee** *as she talks to us:*

Sun-Hee   Accept legal responsibility.

Make a public apology in writing to individual women . . .;

Pay compensation to individual victims . . .;

Make a full disclosure of documents and materials with
regard to comfort stations . . .;

Raise awareness by amending Japanese history books to
reflect historical realities;

Identify and punish perpetrators involved in the
recruitment and institutionalisation of comfort stations
during World War Two.'

Taylor *looks at* **Sun-Hee**. *He bows to her, she doesn't react. She
walks offstage. He closes the file. He looks at us, lets out a huge belly
laugh.*

Taylor   She did it. She fucking did it! Blasted off the moon.

*A shrill sound of telephone ringing. His face freezes. He picks up the
phone, clutching the report. He listens . . .*

Yes, sir. Report's pretty damning.

Listens.

There's no mention whatsoever of our knowledge or, uh, the
whore houses in Japan.

Listens.

We ride it out, sir, that's what we do. For as long as it takes.
(*Listens.*) 'Til they're all dead and forgotten.

Listens.

Oh yeah, Priyanka's a tough cookie. Woulda been a good
recruit, heh heh . . .

Listens.

Boy, she's hot. (*Laughs, listens.*) No sir, I did not! Gentlemen
prefer blondes, right sir? (*His expression is wrought with guilt.*)

OK.

Taylor *laughs as he hangs up the phone. His expression immediately
softens. He rubs his eyes, sighs.*

Sorry, girls . . . Like I said, we got on this moon first.

He tosses away the report. Walks away in a sombre mood.

Epilogue

2018. Video: A coffin carried by demonstrators in front of the Japanese Embassy in Seoul. Broadcast: 'The first woman who spoke out as a wartime "comfort woman", **Kim Sun-Hee***, has died aged ninety-one. Only twenty-four survivors are alive today in South Korea.'*

During **Sun-Hee***'s funeral procession.*

Yuna   Excuse me, you are the U.N. person? Priyanka Silva?

Priyanka (*smiles*)   I'm no longer with the U.N. Too much white tape.

Yuna   My father . . . You met him. Maybe you remember. Han Min?

Priyanka (*stunned*)   You must be . . . Yuna.

Yuna   Yes. You knew my father! (*Beat.*) He passed away a while ago.

Priyanka *gazes at* **Yuna**. *She hesitates for a long moment.*

Priyanka   I knew your mother too. (*She looks at the passing coffin.*)

The women talk but we don't hear their spoken words. **Yuna** *listens in astonishment, she shakes her head. Her head drops as she weeps.*

TRANSITION: Montage of video and audio reports.

Nadia Murad, a former sexual slave of the Islamic State (IS) forces in Iraq, is the co-recipient of the 2018 Nobel Peace Prize 'for their efforts to end the use of sexual violence as a weapon of war and armed conflict'.

2005: The Asian Women's Fund set up to aid former 'comfort women' will be dissolved as many victims rejected the Fund because it neither came directly from the Japanese government nor was accompanied by an official government apology.

2007: Japan's Prime Minister Abe provoked fury when he told reporters regarding the so-called 'comfort women', 'There was no evidence of coercion as initially suggested . . . We have to take it from there.'

2007: The Associated Press review of historical records show that Japan set up a similar 'comfort women' station for American G.I.s until the spring of 1946.

2017: First known video of 'comfort women' during World War Two, an 18-second black-and-white clip taken by a U.S.-Army private, found after a 2-year hunt in U.S. archives.

2019: ACLED records over 100 government-perpetrated sexual violence events since the beginning of 2018 . . . 95% of sexual violence events in which the gender of the victim is reported target women or girls . . .

2021: Human Rights Pulse report. Sexual exploitation in the UK has increased significantly from 2017-2020 . . . The NRM discovered that the most prevalent type of exploitation for children was sexual, including forced prostitution.

2022: The Chinese deputy permanent representative to the U.N. said in an appeal to the Security Council, 'We solemnly urge Japan to face up to and reflect on its history of aggression, handle issues left over from history, such as the forced drafting of "comfort women", in a responsible manner, bring justice to the victims and survivors . . .'

2022: Global Citizen report. (The U.S. Supreme Court overturning of Roe vs Wade) 'goes beyond politics; women's choices and freedoms are threatened. Women will be prosecuted for making a decision about their bodies'.

2022: A Hankyoreh news report: 'With Kim Yang-Ju's passing, only 11 survivors registered with the (South) Korean government are still living.'

Video: Rallying and chanting of ongoing Wednesday Demonstration in Seoul.

Final image of **Sun-Hee***'s statue cast in bronze: 2011. 'Japan has expressed outrage of a bronze statue depicting a young girl that has been placed in front of its embassy in Seoul. The Statue of Peace is a symbol of sexual slavery that women endured during World War Two.'*

End.

Acknowledgements

My gratitude to:

The three women who inspired the play - Kim Hak-soon, Radhika Coomaraswamy and Nadia Murad.

My husband, Christophe, and our sons, ASL and LHL.

Georgina Ruffhead, my phenomenal agent at The Haworth Agency. The team at New Earth Theatre, its AD and my (self-designated) mentor, Kumiko Mendl. Lee Yong-soo, our brief encounter profoundly reshaped my thinking of 'survivor'. Ria Parry, whose aura makes the room so special. Emily Ling Williams and Alexandra Kataigida, for among many things, their forensic eyes. TK Hay for his set vision, Erin Guan, the exquisiteness of costume, Jamie Lu, the Sound No. 1, Gillian Tan and Jeni Seo. Every individual in the artistic and production teams. Caroline Jester for her unwavering belief and John Hoggarth – John, I'll never lose those three keys to playwriting. Jessie Baek, Kwong Loke, Sarah Lam, Sharan Phull, Ross Armstrong and Minhee Yeo for their intrepidity and questions that enriched the script (special thanks to Minhee's mother). Suki Mok for the evocative photos. Emily McLaughlin, Nina Steiger and Stewart Pringle at the National Theatre Studio, 2018–19. The actors who took part in the sharing at the National Theatre Studio, the Soho Theatre reading and the VoiceOver recordings. Dom O'Hanlon, Jonnie Nash and the indefatigable Judy Tither at Methuen Drama and Bloomsbury Academic. Rebecca Bullamore at Kate Morley PR. My friends for their encouragement and the many walks on Hampstead Heath. Steffi, for whom I have an unhealthy and unreciprocated obsession. And Arcola Theatre, the place of firsts for me.

Finally, Lisa Goldman, whose phone call that night in 2017 started this journey.

For a complete listing of
Methuen Drama titles, visit:

www.bloomsbury.com/drama

Follow us on Twitter and keep up to date
with our news and publications

@MethuenDrama